SILVER CITY AIRWAYS

SILVER CITY AIRWAYS
PIONEERS OF THE SKIES

KEITH J. DAGWELL

The
History
Press

This book is dedicated to the memory of my father, H.G. Dagwell, and to all Silver City and associated companies' staff, including support companies at all Silver City bases.

First published 2010

The History Press
The Mill, Brimscombe Port
Stroud, Gloucestershire, GL5 2QG
www.thehistorypress.co.uk

British Library Cataloguing in Publication Data.
A catalogue record for this book is available from the British Library.

ISBN 978 0 7524 5362 0

Typesetting and origination by The History Press
Printed in Great Britain
Manfacturing managed by Jellyfish Print Solutions Ltd

CONTENTS

FOREWORD

By CAPTAIN DAVID FLETT QCVSA
Fleet Manager, Silver City Airways 1954–1962

'Silver City Airways: what a strange name to call a small charter airline' was the remark frequently heard from the passengers. The name was derived from the mining town of Broken Hill, Australia, because of the huge quantities of silver, lead and zinc extracted from the Zinc Corporation Mine. The connection with the Zinc Corporation was established when its directors put up the money to buy four ex-RAF Dakotas and three new Avro Lancastrians on the advice of their air advisor, Air Commodore Griffith Powell, who became Silver City's managing director.

Air Commodore Powell was an ex-senior captain with Imperial Airways who was placed in charge of the North Atlantic Ferry Command during the war, delivering hundreds of American-built 'Lend-Lease' aircraft for the RAF.

The Dakotas were mainly engaged on charter freight and passenger flights in Europe and the Lancastrians on long-range flights for the Zinc Corporation, carrying staff and supplies between the company's far-flung mining operations.

In 1947 the Indian sub-continent was partitioned and the Indian Government chartered a fleet of aircraft, including Dakotas and a Bristol Freighter from Silver City, to move thousands of Hindus back to India from the newly created Pakistan. During the harsh winter of 1947/48, Air Commodore Powell experimented with loading cars into his Bristol Freighter at Blackbushe – his intention being to carry cars across the Channel, avoiding the long queues at Dover. He chose the Kent airfield of Lympne to operate the forty-seven-mile, twenty-minute flight to the French coastal town of Le Touquet. The appropriate licences were obtained from the authorities and the first commercial crossing took place on 14 July 1948. Agreements were concluded with the AA and the RAC, resulting in an avalanche of bookings.

In 1953, Silver City took delivery of new, larger Bristol Superfreighters in order to cope with the increased demand. Owing to the operational restrictions of Lympne, they commissioned a new airport to be built on the Dungeness promontory near the town of Lydd. Operations began there in the spring of 1954, with up to 110 flights leaving for the Continent on busy weekends in July and August. In addition, services ran from Southampton, although these were later moved to Bournemouth.

Although car ferries were the core business, the company opened up many more operations. The Passenger Division at Lydd was busily engaged flying package tour holiday groups on Dakotas to several European resorts. A coach–rail–air service from London to Paris was started under the grand title of the Silver Arrow at a competitive price of £8 0s 0d. During the mid-fifties, Silver City bought-out several smaller companies including Air Kruise, Aquila Airways, Lancashire Aircraft Corporation and Manx Airlines and they began operations at Blackpool and the Isle of Man with routes to Northern Ireland and Scotland.

In 1956 they were awarded the Cumberbatch Trophy – the prestigious air-safety award. In the same year, the Duke of Edinburgh officially opened Lydd but, as the end of the decade approached, Air Commodore Powell's health deteriorated and he was forced to resign. The aircraft were ageing and needed more maintenance. The sea ferries had become much larger and competition was increasing. It was essential to have larger aircraft carrying more cars at a cheaper price, but the cost of building such specialised aircraft was prohibitive. There was also additional competition from Air Charter, operating a similar service from their base at Southend but, in 1960, they were amalgamated into the UK's new independent carrier British United Airways.

In 1962, the principal shareholders of Silver City sold the company and it, too, became part of British United Airways, thus marking the end of Silver City Airways. The cross-Channel air ferry continued under the names of British United Air Ferries and then British Air Ferries until January 1971, when the last car ferry service left Lydd for Le Touquet. Many a tear was shed by the dedicated Silver City staff and so ended an innovative service that was loved by the British motoring public.

David Flett
Bishop's Cleeve
Gloucestershire
June 2009

PREFACE

I joined Silver City Airways at Ferryfield (Lydd) Airport direct from the RAF in 1958; my job was an Instrument Engineer working on the Bristol Freighters and DC3s. Ten years later, I left British United Air Ferries (as it had then become) and joined the parent company as an Avionics Inspector on VC-10s and BAC 1-11s at their Gatwick base.

Annual Silver City reunions had been held at Gatwick, or in that area, since 1977; in 1987 I was asked to take over the organisation of this event which I have done ever since, developing it into the Silver City Association. Some years ago, I was invited to talk to a Royal Air Forces Association (RAFA) group about Silver City. This proved to be quite popular; the word spread and I made quite a number of presentations to various organisations. During these events, it was suggested several times that I should write a book. At the time this seemed a daunting task but the Silver City Association members encouraged me to produce something that was a record of the unique company operations.

In partnership with Colin van Geffen (graphics and editing) and Alina Jenkins (narration), I produced a 'talking book' CD called *The Silver City Story* which was well received by the media but with comments on how much better it would be as a book! Encouraged by these comments, here is the book: *Silver City Airways*.

Unless credited otherwise, the pictures used in this book have been provided by the Silver City Association (www.silvercityairways.com) or Reflections Images (www.relections-images.co.uk). Other contributions are courtesy of: Audrey Kennard; *The Kentish Express*; The Aviation Hobby Shop; Mick (Timber) Wood; David Hedges (who kindly provided much of the information used to compile the Fleet Lists); Shell; Phil Rix; Mike Hooks; Angus Cameron; and LAT Photographic (Auto Sport).

My special thanks go to Paul Ross (editing) and Ken Honey (photographic reproduction); without their help this book could not have been produced.

Keith J. Dagwell
Worthing
West Sussex
July 2009

CHAPTER 1

WHY 'SILVER CITY'?

The question that is most often asked is: Why 'Silver City'? To answer this involves going back to the early days of a company called British Aviation Services Ltd, from which all this developed. It is, therefore, as good a starting point as any to introduce the Silver City Airways story.

British Aviation Services was formed at the end of 1945 by the shareholders of the British Aviation Insurance Co. Its purpose was to provide technical services to aviation and, in particular, to the insurance interests in aviation.

The managing director was Air Commodore Griffith Powell – usually known as 'Taffy'. With him initially were several ex-RAF people who had served with him in Ferry Command and subsequently in Transport Command.

For most of the war, Powell was based in Montreal and was primarily responsible for the ferrying of American-built aircraft to Europe, Africa and the Middle East. Before the war he had been a pilot with Imperial Airways, flying such aircraft as the Handley Page HP42 in and out of Croydon Airport.

Taffy's team shared two small offices in London's Lime Street. Taffy and a secretary had one office, the others sat around a table in the other room sharing a telephone and generally making life miserable for the real tenants who had discovered, too late, their error in subletting the space.

Imagine the confusion that prevailed at times during those early days when arrangements were being made to ferry a large number of war surplus aircraft, involving the employment of over one hundred surplus aircrew, all of whom used to come to the office either to be interviewed or to get their flight briefings. At that time, many of them had not yet become adjusted to civilian life.

Among the various tasks that British Aviation Services undertook was to re-equip the Turkish Air Force with some 300 Spitfires and Mosquitoes – but their first job was to act as technical advisers to Alberto Dodero, an Argentine shipping magnate who proposed to start an air service between Buenos Aires and Montevideo. He purchased five ex-military Short Sunderland flying boats and had them converted to 'Sandringhams' which offered lavish passenger accommodation. British Aviation Services delivered the Sandringhams to Buenos Aires. A party of Dodero's personal friends went along on each of the delivery flights, which proved to be an important element in Silver City's history.

On one of these delivery flights was John Govett, chairman of the Zinc Corporation and a man of wide and important business interests. The Zinc Corporation was a big mining company with its headquarters in England; its principal mines were in Australia with a host of associations all over the world.

At that time – late 1945 and early 1946 – the mining companies were working hard to restore properties that in many cases had been allowed to run down during the war years. This frequently involved the movement of large groups of technicians and their equipment. Unfortunately, the airlines were still in their infancy and passenger space was always difficult to obtain. Among these large companies with worldwide interests, there was a real need for some means of fast transport under their own control.

As a result of John Govett's introduction to British Aviation Services plus the Dodero flights and travel requirements of the Zinc Corporation (with its associated interests), a company was formed to provide transportation and to act as a general charter company. The managers were to be British Aviation Services who also had a small shareholding in the new company. The directors were John Govett, W.S. Robinson and Air Commodore Powell. The name chosen was Silver City Airways.

The reason for the choice was simple: the Zinc Corporation's principal mines (producing lead and zinc) were at the small town of Broken Hill in New South Wales, Australia. The town is known to every Australian as 'Silver City' – a reminder of the days when it was principally a silver mine; they needed to look no further for a name.

There is a curious footnote to this story. At about this time, there appeared in a London shop a great display of packets of something called 'Silver City Shredded Beef Suet'. Enquiries were made of the manufacturers (located in Aberdeen) to ask how it was that they were using the name Silver City. The response was that the suet had been packed under that name for twenty years. Apparently, the name 'Silver City' had been applied to Aberdeen since ancient times, long before the present name of 'Granite City' came into popular use.

Silver City Airways was formally registered on 25 November 1946 and purchased seven aircraft – three new Avro Lancastrians and four Douglas DC3 Dakotas bought from the US Foreign Liquidation Commission. All the aircraft were configured to a high level of passenger comfort.

The Lancastrian was basically a converted Lancaster bomber, the major changes being the removal of the three gun turrets and bomb bay, trimming the interior and fitting between nine and thirteen passenger seats. The baggage was stowed through a hinged section of the aircraft's new streamlined nose.

The first Lancastrian charter flight was from London Airport (Heathrow) on 24 October 1946 under the command of Captain John Adams, with Roy Day as his co-pilot. The round trip to Australia took fourteen days, routing via London–Johannesburg–Sydney with refuelling stops en-route. Although fourteen days was the scheduled time, this was quite often exceeded due to weather or technical delays; sometimes both.

The Dakotas carried about thirty passengers. One of them purchased from the RAF was named *City of Hollywood* and was the best executive Dakota in Europe. It had eight Rumbold reclining seats – enormous things that resembled plush barbers' chairs. In addition to these there were two settees and a bar.

Lancastrian flights to Australia and South Africa began before the end of 1946, initially operating from Langley Airfield in Buckinghamshire before moving to the growing London Airport at Heathrow.

In those early years, a lot of flying was done both for the Zinc Corporation and in general charter. Silver City acquired a DC4 Skymaster which carried out a number of round-the-world trips – many on behalf of the Zinc Corporation. Also in this period, Silver City carried out the first of what proved to be many flights carrying Mr Winston Churchill (as he then was). The DC3 *City of Hollywood* was the preferred aircraft; whenever Churchill had flown in this aircraft there was a great rush to grab one of his cigar ends from the capacious ashtray. The cigar bands had his name on them and so became highly prized souvenirs.

On the operational front, business was brisk. The company formed another offshoot – British Aviation Services (Malta). This operated three Airspeed Consuls, each capable of carrying about six passengers to various points throughout the Mediterranean area.

Aircraft ferrying was very intensive with the company making many flights, including flying military DC3s and DC4s from Europe to refurbishment companies such as Canadair in Canada and then flying the shining civil conversions back to their European customers. In addition, Catalina flying boats were delivered to the Far East.

Aircraft engineering and maintenance were playing a big part in British Aviation Services' business at this time, too. A large engineering base had been opened at Blackbushe Airport near Camberley, Surrey, in 1946 and in early 1947 maintenance of the Silver City Lancastrian and Dakota fleets was undertaken at this facility, along with maintenance work for other aircraft operators.

At the end of 1947, political events in India could in some ways be considered as the next decisive step in the future Air Ferry's development. The country's partition had resulted in a mass migration of Hindus from the newly formed Pakistan to India and of Muslims in the opposite direction. An airlift was organised in September; Silver City scented business (Powell had a well-developed nose for this) and the Dakotas were duly despatched to India.

The Dakotas were able to carry thirty to forty passengers and, as might be imagined, Taffy would have loved to have stretched those aircraft. However, he found out that one of the newly developed Bristol 170 Freighter demonstrators was idle at Filton, near Bristol, and had a better idea. After some rapid talks with the manufacturers, the Bristol Aeroplane Company, the aircraft – a Mark II Wayfarer registered G-AHJC – was winging its way to India. Soon this aircraft was to set up a record of lifting 1,105 people and their baggage in nine days.

Although the aircraft was only certified by the British airworthiness authorities to carry forty people, dispensation had been given for the seats and fittings to be removed and on one flight it carried 119 people. A second Mk IIA 170 (G-AHJG) was leased from

Bristols and joined the airlift in early 1948. According to Bristols' advertisements at the time, the authorised all-up weight of 37,000lb was not exceeded!

The Bristol Type 170 Freighter was developed in 1944 as a design suitable for quick production for the post-war market and first flew on 2 December 1945. Most of the early versions of this aircraft did not have big opening nose doors and were therefore used for passengers or small freight that could go through the normal passenger door; these versions were called 'Wayfarers'. The bulk of the Freighters, however, were built or modified to have the big fully opening 'clamshell' nose doors. These later became known as the Mk 21 or 'short-nose' Freighters. The aircraft was quite large with a wingspan of 108ft (6ft more than a Lancaster bomber) and a length of 68ft. It cruised at 165mph and its top speed was 195mph. The fuselage was square in section, permitting loads of two Rolls-Royce-size cars in the cargo hold and seats for twelve passengers in the rear. With the aircraft intended for low-speed operations over relatively short distances, there was no need for a retractable undercarriage and so a fixed undercarriage was provided.

The large wings carried 700 gallons of fuel. The Mk 21 version was powered by two Bristol Hercules radial piston engines each producing 1,690hp. The aircraft was initially operated with the pilot in the left-hand seat; a radio operator being the second crew member. Later it became a two-pilot operation with the radio operator's duties having been absorbed by the pilots. The radio operator's seat in the rear of the cockpit therefore became spare. The Bristol Freighter was an all-British design and 214 aircraft of all Marks were built.

This then was Silver City's first acquaintance with the Bristol 170 which ripened into a beautiful friendship. From this initial experience came the talks which led to the creation of the Air Ferry. At this time, Bristols had another Freighter demonstrator in North America and one of its 'party tricks' was to load some cars into the hold and make a demonstration flight, much publicised in America at the time. This demonstration was not lost on Taffy, as one of his favourite pastimes was to take his large Armstrong Siddeley Lancaster car (HXN 88) touring in France. At that time, this involved driving to a Channel port, having the fuel drained from the car and then watching it being craned onto the deck of the ship – plus, of course, the mass of paperwork and the horror for him of having to queue! All this took a long time and the journey to France could take many hours. Patience was not one of Taffy's strong points and he had suddenly seen a way to reduce this to a little over an hour. One thing led to another and in 1948 Silver City ferried this demonstration aircraft back from Montreal and the stage was set for the start of the Air Ferry.

In the early months of 1948, British Aviation Services had formed Northern Rhodesia Aviation Services which flew Airspeed Consuls, supported by a Silver City de Havilland Dove and Bristol 170 on internal routes. In the summer of that year, Silver City won a lucrative contract with the French racehorse owner Marcel Boussac to fly him around Europe in either a Dove or the VIP Dakota.

By late 1948 it was apparent that one of the original reasons for forming the company – to provide worldwide transport for its owners, the Zinc Corporation – was no longer necessary, because by that time the airlines had improved and grown considerably. The total shareholding of Silver City Airways was therefore acquired by its original managers who by now rejoiced in the name of Britavia, which thus became Silver City's new parent company.

While the formation of Silver City was going on, British Aviation Services had been busy in their own right: a move to three floors of No.1 Great Cumberland Place near Marble Arch being just one of their activities.

Right: Air Commodore 'Taffy' Powell.

Below: Silver City Lancastrian
G-AHBW *City of London.*

15

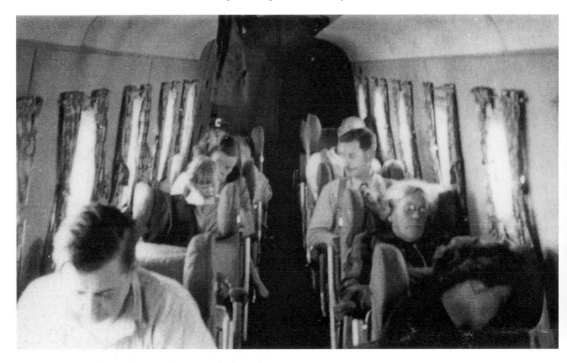

The interior of a Silver City Lancastrian en-route from London to Sydney.

A Silver City Lancastrian just prior to departure.

Right: Mr Winston Churchill (as he then was) returning to the UK from Marrakesh in 1947 with his wife Clementine. The Silver City DC3 G-AJAV *City of Hollywood* was used for the flight.

Below: An Airspeed Consul similar to this was used by British Aviation Services (Malta) in 1946; its registration was G-AIBF.

Bristol 170 Mk II Wayfarer G-AHJC – the Bristol demonstrator – seen here at Blackbushe in 1947. A civil Short Stirling V can be seen in the background. These transports – developed from the Stirling bomber – were used by the Belgian charter company Trans-Air (later Air Transport) on the Blackbushe–Shanghai route but were not very successful.

Bristol 170 Mk 21 G-AIFV at Lympne in the early 1950s. The picture clearly shows the general arrangement of the type.

Right: Len Madelaine with the Lockheed Lodestar G-AJAW; it was used to return crews from delivery flights.

Below: British Aviation Services staff at Blackbushe in 1947 with the Lockheed Lodestar.

CHAPTER 2

THE AIR FERRY EMERGES

The first Silver City car ferry operation – the proving flight between Lympne in Kent and Le Touquet on the French coast – took place on 15 June 1948. (Some reports put this date as 7 July but a crew member's log book shows 15 June.) The aircraft was Bristol 170 G–AGVC, the same aircraft that had carried out the North American demonstrations. It was commanded by Captain Ian Cochrane with a radio operator in the co-pilot's seat. An engineer – Leo 'Spud' Murphy – was also on board and keeping a close eye on the flight was 'Taffy' Powell himself. Nobody was exceptionally enthusiastic about the venture and certainly no one had any idea what it would lead to.

Lympne and Le Touquet were chosen as the two terminals for the simple reason that there were no other existing cross-Channel civil airports quite so close together. The distance was forty-seven miles which was nearly twice as far as the shortest sea crossing. Lympne was an old First World War airfield situated on the hills overlooking Romney Marsh. There was only one car on that first flight – Air Commodore Powell's Armstrong Siddeley Lancaster.

Naturally the insurers had been advised of the flight and Captain Lamplugh of the British Aviation Insurance Co. had gone on ahead to greet the pioneers at Le Touquet. It is said that he went there mainly to see what the effect on the aeroplane would be 'if and when' the car fell out over the Channel! However, the flight took place without incident and, twenty minutes after leaving Lympne, Taffy's car was safely decanted onto French soil. The aircraft also carried its own loading ramp which had to be put in place to offload the car.

Then at Le Touquet a most remarkable thing happened. Another English visitor – Sammy Norman – found himself in the unfortunate position of having both his personal aircraft and his Bentley there at the same time (there were such people even then) and the arrival of the Bristol 170 relieved him of a dilemma. Silver City agreed to fly the Bentley home for 300,000 old Francs – 'cash in advance' – paid to Taffy. In the excitement of the moment, nobody stopped to ask about the length of the Bentley and a rather delicate situation arose when it seemed as if a choice had to be made between the Bentley and Taffy's Armstrong Siddeley. However, both cars were somehow loaded – although there was no more than 1in to spare when the nose doors were closed. (The aircraft doors were later modified to give an extra 18in of space.)

After this initial and quite unexpected financial coup, it was felt safe to expose this radical new idea to the Press as well as to the motoring associations. The inaugural flight took off from Lympne on 14 July 1948 which, appropriately enough, was Bastille Day in France. The aircraft was commanded by Captain 'Storm' Clarke, a Lancastrian veteran who had come to Silver City from British South American Airways; his co-pilot was Jerry Rosser.

At this time, Silver City had no licence to operate a scheduled service either across the Channel or, indeed, anywhere else. The Civil Aviation Act, which reserved practically everything for the three state-owned corporations – British European Airways (BEA), British Overseas Airways (BOAC) and British South American Airways (BSAA), which merged with BOAC in 1949 – was an ever-present threat to the independent charter companies. More than one flight a month between the same two places could be classified as a 'scheduled service' (unless it could be proved to be a bona-fide charter flight). Large fines and possible imprisonment awaited the offender. The Air Ferry therefore started on a charter basis with most flights being taken by the RAC and the AA. However, the very first charter booking (excluding the Bentley windfall) was from ex-Queen Ramphaiphanni of Siam (now Thailand). The fare from Lympne to Le Touquet was £27 0s 0d (equivalent to over £700 today) for a medium-sized car and up to four passengers, or £32 0s 0d (more than £850 today) for a large car and passengers.

The facilities at both ends of the route were no more than adequate. At Lympne there was one van which served all the office and traffic functions and one man – Bob 'Mac' McRae – combined the duties of receptionist, traffic officer, car loader and whatever else was wanted. He was granted the use of the telephone in the Ministry of Civil Aviation's police box (no Tardis this) although this was subject to the prior claims of the constabulary. Customs examination and clearance of the cars was conducted in a corner of the field, open to the elements but fenced round to deter the attentions of the sheep (which in the first year were more numerous than the passengers).

At Le Touquet, the situation was much the same although there was a concrete runway there which was more than could be said for Lympne. The check-in procedure at Lympne was simple; the passenger would park his or her car, present the documentation and ticket sent to them by the motoring association concerned and then, when called, proceed to the customs clearance point. Remember that, at this time, the Bristol 170 Mk 21 could carry just two large cars and twelve passengers. Once cleared, the car would be collected by a Silver City loader-driver, then driven up the ramp (placed at the nose of the aircraft) and into the hold where it would be shackled down.

When the cars were loaded and the nose doors closed, the passengers would be taken out to the aircraft by the ground hostess. They boarded through a door in the port (left) side of the aircraft and were seated in the small cabin which was located to the rear of the car hold. Cars and passengers were separated by a bulkhead with a small door in it to allow access to the cars, if necessary, by the car marshal who made up the third member of the crew. The flight crew of two would have already climbed up the ladder inside the hold and taken their seats on the flight deck. Engines would be started and the aircraft would taxy out to the end of the runway for take-off. Ninety minutes were allowed for a round trip including loading, unloading and refuelling if required. The average flying and taxying time was about fifty minutes, which therefore left twenty minutes at each end for all the ground services.

When the numbers were counted at the end of that first season, Silver City had carried 170 cars, quite surprising in view of the cumbersome 'charter' arrangements that had to be negotiated. No really serious problems had shown themselves. The worst problem – apart from keeping the operation within the rules – was that of shackling the cars down in the hold. This had proved to be a very time-consuming task. A few years later, the solution was to be found by one of Silver City's own staff.

Bert Hayes was a young man from Folkestone who had a yearning to fly. He joined the RAF and was trained to fly Hurricanes. When the war ended, he was discharged from the RAF with only a few flying hours. There was little work, particularly for a pilot with low experience, so he took a job as a van driver. One day he saw an advertisement for a loader-driver with Silver City at Lympne. He applied and got the job. He enjoyed his work but still had the burning ambition to fly again. Part of Bert's job was to shackle the cars down and he too was irritated by the time it took. He gave the matter a great deal of thought and came up with a design for a device which fitted between the chains and the floor of the aircraft.

The device could tighten the shackles merely by moving one lever and release them just as quickly. He had a prototype manufactured and called it a 'Shacklip'. Bert saw his opportunity and went to the Silver City management offering his 'Shacklip' to the company in exchange for them training him to get his commercial pilot's licence. The company agreed and in the coming months and years the devices saved hours in turn-around time. As for Bert, before very long he had passed his exams and could regularly be seen resplendent in his pilot's uniform proudly walking out to the Bristol aircraft.

Towards the end of 1948, permission was sought from the Ministry of Civil Aviation to operate a scheduled car ferry service between Lympne and Le Touquet. This involved Silver City entering into an Associate Agreement with BEA, which was the required procedure at that time. This arrangement took time to put in place but, on 2 May 1949, the licence to operate one year's scheduled service (covering the whole of 1949) was eventually signed. Thus began the first year of scheduled Air Ferry operations.

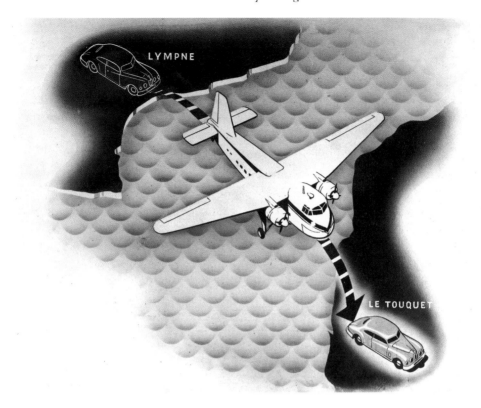

The first car ferry route – Lympne to Le Touquet.

Bristol 170 Freighter with an Armstrong Siddeley Lancaster – similar to Taffy Powell's. The early individual ramps are being put into position.

Left: The first colour brochure advertising the car ferry, 1948.

Right: A 1949 brochure showing the fares at that time.

ALL-INCLUSIVE CAR FERRY SERVICE TO THE CONTINENT

Your car, luggage, and up to four passengers . .

- Lympne (Folkestone)—Le Touquet

  £27 for cars up to 14 ft. overall length per single journey

  £32 for cars over 14 ft. overall length per single journey

- No extra charge for children not occupying seats.

- Supplement of £2 2s. for adults in excess of 4 per car.

- Personal service and attention.

- Special rates on request for motor-cycles, other vehicles and livestock.

- Cars are driven directly on and off Bristol Freighter aircraft.

- Passengers are accommodated in separate cabin at rear of aircraft.

Hourly and Half Hourly Services from both Termini

An overhead view of Lympne airport in 1952. Romney Marsh is in the background.

Two passengers pose with their car at Lympne in 1950.

Above: Two passengers about to board a Bristol 170 Mk 21 at Lympne in 1950.

Left: The 'Shacklip', the device invented by Silver City pilot Bert Hayes.

Staff at a rainy Blackbushe in 1948; note the Silver City Airspeed Consul (right) and a Miles Aerovan to the left.

Staff outing from Blackbushe in an early Silver City DC3.

CHAPTER 3

THE AIR FERRY SPREADS ITS WINGS

Before looking at 1949 and the Air Ferry side of things, it is first necessary to make a slight diversion eastwards – to Germany. In the autumn of 1948, Russian actions led to the Berlin Airlift, in which both civil and military aircraft were engaged. Silver City joined in with a single Bristol 170 in September and because that aircraft proved itself especially useful with large single package loads, the company leased further Freighters from Bristols and added these to the Airlift. Altogether they used four Freighters, although never more than two at a time. When the Airlift scaled down in February 1949, Silver City's Freighters were the last civil twin-engined aircraft there – having flown a total of about 800 hours. One aircraft – G-AGVB – set up a twin-engined aircraft record by carrying 34 tons to Hamburg in the course of one day.

The Freighter was by no means a handsome aircraft and some American pilots taunted the Silver City crews over the airwaves with jibes like 'Gee – did you make that yourself?' or, having heard Air Traffic give clearance to a Wayfarer (remember the early Freighters were called 'Wayfarers'), by asking 'Did you say the *Mayflower*?'

Whatever else, in 1949 Silver City started the first scheduled year of Air Ferry services with a considerable amount of operating experience on the Bristol 170. Nothing from previous years indicated what volume of traffic might be expected at this stage, neither of the two motoring organisations being particularly enthusiastic. During 1949, Silver City did what they could to improve facilities at both ends of the route. At Lympne, 'Mac' McRae moved into an office in the Ministry of Civil Aviation building; this at least relieved him of the need to maintain good relations with the police to preserve his telephone service. However, customs clearance was still done in the open air.

In February, so as to 'legalise' the operation in France, Silver City registered a new company in Paris – Société Commerciale Aérienne du Littoral (SCAL). Silver City began the season in April with three Bristol 170s, none of which they owned, and the bookings during the first few weeks gave no cause for dancing in the streets. Three return trips a day were advertised. During these lean winter months, the company needed the aircraft to continue earning their keep; racehorses and livestock became frequent cargoes. In particular, Malta needed high-quality cattle to restore her depleted stock and four flights to the island were undertaken in April.

However, in June bookings started rolling in at a rapid rate and continued to do so until August, by which time the company was sometimes operating more than twenty round trips a day! By August that year, Silver City were doing really substantial business, so much so that a further two Bristol 170s were hired for a short period to cope with the traffic which was largely concentrated at weekends. At the end of the season, Silver City were still operating three Bristol 170s which had carried 2,600 cars, one hundred motorcycles and a total of 7,900 accompanying passengers.

Everything the company heard from users of the service encouraged them to believe that the operation could be substantially developed. In October 1949, a system of route licensing through the Air Transport Advisory Council had been introduced. The company applied for an extension of the Lympne to Le Touquet route for between three to five years – but they were granted just two years. The company then announced that the fares would be cut for the next year's operations. The Air Ferry saw a lot of prestige cars among their customers' vehicles, a notable traveller in October 1950 being Mr Anthony Crook, a thirty-year-old Caterham racing motorist and Bristol car agent driving a two-litre Bristol 401. Crook took off from Lympne at 7.15a.m. on 12 October and arrived at Le Touquet at 7.50a.m. He then drove 170 miles to the famous racing circuit at Montlhery via Paris. Crook's Bristol completed eighty-seven laps of the saucer-shaped track (104.78 miles) in one hour, thus setting a new record for a two-litre car. The car registration was aptly MPH 100. Anthony Crook is still a well-known Bristol agent in London.

It became clear that the practice of charging an inclusive rate for a vehicle and up to four passengers was not popular. The man travelling with only his wife took understandable exception to paying the same fare as another car with four passengers. Up to that time, the terms of their licence precluded the company from carrying passengers without a vehicle. 'Taffy' saw this as a dreadful loss of potential revenue and having determined that a bicycle was a 'vehicle', arranged for bicycles to be stationed at both Lympne and Le Touquet for single passengers to hire, thus skirting round the problem. The cash registers rang again! Things got even better when he read of a High Court action involving a claim for damages in a street accident where the learned judge ruled that a man on roller skates was guilty of not being in control of his *vehicle*. However, it was not necessary to supply roller skates to potential passengers because the issue quietly went away. Silver City ended 1949 with a profit of £4,520.

1950 was very much a repetition of the previous year but with a steady increase in traffic. The year saw the appearance in modest quantities of two new classes of traffic – motorcycles and pedal cycles, which from then on provided a substantial proportion of the traffic. Later in the operations, 'pedal cycle specials' were laid on when thirty-six seats were put into the Freighter's hold together with the cyclists' machines; with no sound insulation it was a bit noisy but no one seemed to care. In previous years, the operation had ended in the autumn but in 1950 operations continued through the winter.

The final traffic figures for 1950 were:

3,253 cars carried;

639 motorcycles carried;

127 pedal cycles carried; and

10,800 passengers carried.

At the same time that the decision was made to operate during the winter, Silver City made a new application for a five-year licence, which was considered the minimum time needed for any long-term planning and fleet expansion. The licence was granted in the early part of 1951 for the continuation of the Lympne to Le Touquet route and a new route from Lympne to Ostend, although this route was not flown until the following year.

So the position at the beginning of 1951 was this: the company had a five-year licence, a reasonably substantial set-up at both ends of the route, some enthusiastic sales agents, five Bristol 170s and a good number of satisfied customers. The fares too were altered: cars were between £16 0s 0d (equivalent to £380 today) and £24 0s 0d (£580) depending on length; motorcycles were £3 0s 0d (over £70 today) for a solo and £5 0s 0d (£120) for a combination; pedal cycles were £1 (£24) and passengers were £2 (£48) each way. These new lower fares, combined with a rise to £100 (some £2,400 today) in the Foreign Currency Allowance (the amount of cash travellers were allowed to take out of the country), set the scene for what was to be a bumper year.

Among the outstanding features of the year was the aircraft efficiency. With just six aircraft (an additional 170 having joined the fleet in July), Silver City was able to operate as many as forty-eight round trips on some peak days. This meant that each aircraft was making up to sixteen take-offs and landings a day – and only during daylight hours. Two more 170s were acquired from the French company Société Commerciale Aérienne du Littoral.

It was becoming apparent that a second route to the Continent could well be another good source of revenue. After careful thought it was decided that Southampton (Eastleigh) to Cherbourg (Maupertus), a distance of eighty-eight miles with a flight time of thirty-five minutes, had the right potential. Southampton offered good access from the Midlands and the West and the port offered great opportunities for freight business. One of those 'opportunities' came to fruition when Silver City linked up with the American Automobile Association to provide a service that would pick up American visitors' cars from the docks and take them to Lympne or Eastleigh for the Air Ferry to fly them to their Continental destinations, where they would be reunited with their owners. The licence for the route was granted on 5 December 1951 when a demonstration flight took off from Southampton under the command of Captain George Hogarth, the Eastleigh chief pilot. On board were local civic dignitaries. Although this was the first flight, the route was not operated commercially until the following year. Car fares were to be between £15 0s 0d (£360 today) and £27 0s 0d (£650), depending on the length of the vehicle. In late 1952, the duration of the licence was agreed to be for ten years.

Meanwhile, back at Lympne, the Air Ferry was operating at record levels during the summer months although, as the pace slackened towards the end of the summer, it was possible to divert aircraft for other business. The Berlin work was still available, albeit on a scaled-down level, and there was still money to be earned there so one of the 170s was soon on the scene. In the autumn, the company secured two substantial contracts. One was with the Rootes car manufacturing group to deliver new cars that were driven from the factory to Lympne and then via the Air Ferry to Le Touquet from where they would be delivered to agents in France or beyond. The second contract was to fly 1,800 cows that had arrived from Ireland to the Continent over a six-week period; customised pens were fitted into the aircraft's hold to carry the animals in safety and comfort.

A few problems were encountered at Lympne due to the 'soggy' state of the airfield at that time of the year. As a result, some flights had to use West Malling in Kent, Blackbushe in Hampshire or Southend in Essex as alternative departure points, which reduced some of the profit. As the aircraft were usually empty on the return journey, every effort was made to find a load for them. Quite often this would be fruit or cheeses which became quite a frequent and profitable cargo. It is interesting to note that at the peak of the summer operations, Silver City carried more than twice as much cargo to Lympne as all the cargo that went into Heathrow and Northolt put together. Overall, 1951 had proved to be a record-breaking year; the actual statistics being:

> 7,529 cars carried;
> 3,240 motorcycles carried;
> 1,355 pedal cycles carried; and
> 30,137 passengers carried.

This was a particularly good result because the Foreign Currency Allowance had been cut to just £50 in the autumn. The profit for the year was just under £48,000.

The Britavia group meanwhile had added another company to its portfolio in February 1951 – Zambaboard, based in Livingstone, Northern Rhodesia (now Zambia). It produced wallboards for buildings out of wood shavings – although not aviation-related it made a good profit!

One of Silver City's frequent flyers at that time was the well-known Polish concert pianist Stanislaus Niedzelfi. Whenever he was on a European tour he would travel from Lympne with his Buick and a large trailer containing his grand piano – needless to say it filled the hold. It is interesting to note that even in those early years, the Silver City board were discussing the possibility of Air Ferry routes from Jerez to Tangier, Miami to Bermuda and Miami to Havana and Nassau – such was their confidence and vision.

Bristol 170 Mk IIA G-AHJC on the Berlin Airlift, September–November 1948. The aircraft is in the Bristol Aeroplane Co.'s livery on lease to Silver City.

Bristol 170 Mk 21 of Société Commerciale Aérienne du Littoral (SCAL). Silver City had an arrangement with SCAL to 'legalise' the operation in France. It is coincidental that the two companies had the same abbreviation.

Len Gilham leads an Argentinean polo pony from a Bristol 170 Mk 21 at Lympne in 1950.

The Bristol 401 two-litre car that had driven 104.78 miles in one hour. Anthony Crook (right), a thirty-year-old racing motorist from Caterham, with his wife, racing mechanic John Dennis and Courtney Edwards of the *Daily Mail*.

to the continent by SILVER CITY in 20 MINUTES

HOURLY AND HALF-HOURLY SERVICES
OPERATED BETWEEN
LYMPNE (Nr. FOLKESTONE) AND LE TOUQUET

The tariff is based on the unaccompanied vehicle rate per single journey — see table below — plus £2 for each occupant or rider.

● Cars — up to 12' 6" overall ... £16
over 12' 6" to 15' 6" ... £20
over 15' 6" £24

● Motorcycles — Solo £3
Combinations £5

● Cycles — Auto £2
Pedal £1

● Passengers — £2
Children under 14 years ... £1
In Arms ... ... Free

● Rates for other vehicles, trailers and livestock, on application.

Cars are driven directly on and off Bristol Freighter aircraft.

Passengers are accommodated in separate cabin at rear.

SILVER CITY AIRWAYS CAR FERRY

11 GREAT CUMBERLAND PLACE, LONDON, W.1., ENGLAND
Telephone: AMBassador 1611

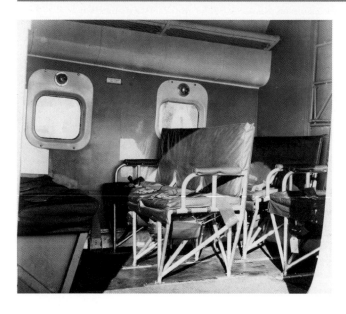

Above: The 1951 combined fares list, timetable and enquiry postcard.

Left: In the early days, the Bristol 170 Mk 21 passenger seating was basic to say the least!

Well-known Polish concert pianist Stanislaus Niedzelfi and his instrument boarding a Bristol 170 Mk 21 at Lympne in 1951.

CHAPTER 4

STANDING ROOM ONLY

In 1952 expectations were running high that Silver City was about to start another great year. The route from Southend to Ostend was started in the spring to give a cross-Channel service to motorists from north of London; however, it was not an immediate success and closed in the autumn, the service moving to Lympne the following year.

Silver City had increased its fleet of 170s to nine aircraft in anticipation of a busy season. In a move to reduce turn-around time, motorised ramps that could be driven up to the aircraft hold by one man replaced the older, heavier ones that needed several people to handle them. In addition, the time-saving was complemented by the introduction of the quick-shackling device – the 'Shacklip' – invented by Bert Hayes and described in Chapter 2.

As the average family was now able to buy a 'family-sized' car, the fares were adjusted again to include a 'small car' category to encourage them to take their vehicle to the continent. Meanwhile in Germany, the Berlin-Hamburg operation was developing into a 'Junior Airlift'. Under a contract with the German government, Silver City released 170s to go there whenever the Air Ferry traffic allowed; indeed, in the autumn as many as five aircraft were operating in Germany.

All was going well when in April the Foreign Currency Allowance was suddenly slashed to £25 0s 0d (about £550 today) which did not go very far on the Continent. The cut spelt disaster for many in the travel industry and it also had its effect on the Air Ferry traffic with bookings dropping below their expected levels. To fill the gaps, some very enterprising and most unusual cargoes were carried. Among them were: Grand National runners; pigeons; lettuces; and tons of furniture for the new NATO headquarters in Brussels.

In spite of this unexpected turn of events, the Southampton to Cherbourg route was well under way. July 1952 saw Silver City reach 10,000 crossings of the Channel without any accidents and the total number of cars carried exceeded 24,000. Silver City also won a contract with the Rootes group to take their new Humber Super Snipe cars for trials at the very hot Tamanrasset in the Algerian Sahara desert. Freighter Mk 21 G-AIFM and a crew comprising Jerry Rosser, Barry Damon, 'Butch' Badger and Len Gilham were the lucky 'volunteers'.

'Taffy' Powell's brain was still as alert as ever for any opportunity to squeeze another 'fare-payer' into any aircraft with an empty space on it. In fact, he put forward the idea that as the flight was only twenty minutes long it was not unreasonable that some passengers could stand; after all, they stood on buses and trains didn't they? He had even devised a safety harness for them! Needless to say, that was one battle he lost with the Ministry.

It was very obvious that the outward and return journey loads did not match up very well; that is to say that although two cars might have gone out, there was no guarantee that two would be waiting to come back. However, if another type of aircraft could be found that had greater capacity with a lower operating cost, the revenue leak could be reduced. The hunt began for a Bristol 170 replacement: a civil double-deck variant of the huge military Blackburn Universal Freighter (subsequently to become the Beverley in RAF service) was considered as it could have carried eight cars and forty passengers, but as there was no certainty of an RAF order or civil production line allocations if a military order did materialise, it was rejected. In the end, Bristols came up with the solution – a stretched version of the 170 which could carry three cars and sixteen passengers. It was known as the Bristol 170 Mk 32, or more familiarly as the 'Superfreighter'.

The main features of the Superfreighter were a lengthening of the hold by 5ft, installation of more powerful Bristol Hercules 734 engines – each giving 2,000hp, an increased fuel capacity of 1,172 gallons and a new Decca navigation system particularly suited to cross-Channel operations. Silver City ordered six of these aircraft at a cost of £90,000 each, to be delivered in the spring of 1953 – the following year.

At the end of 1952 the traffic figures were quite respectable considering the 'bombshell' of the cut in the Foreign Currency Allowance. The traffic figures showed cars and passengers to be about 10 per cent down on 1951, motorcycles were 30 per cent down but pedal cycles were 40 per cent up! Overall, the company had managed to make a profit of £35,000 (equivalent to more than £750,000 today).

SOUTHAMPTON to CHERBOURG — in 35 minutes

One way			Round trip		
£	s.	d.	£	s.	d.
15	0	0	30	0	0
19	0	0	38	0	0
23	0	0	46	0	0
27	0	0	54	0	0
5	0	0	10	0	0
7	0	0	14	0	0
2	10	0	5	0	0
1	5	0	2	10	0
2	0	0	4	0	0
3	15	0	7	10	0
1	17	6	3	15	0
4	0	0	8	0	0

LYMPNE to LE TOUQUET — in 20 minutes

One way			Round trip		
£	s.	d.	£	s.	d.
12	0	0	24	0	0
16	0	0	32	0	0
20	0	0	40	0	0
24	0	0	48	0	0
4	0	0	8	0	0
6	0	0	12	0	0
2	0	0	4	0	0
1	0	0	2	0	0
1	10	0	3	0	0
2	5	0	4	10	0
1	2	6	2	5	0
2	10	0	5	0	0

SOUTHEND to OSTEND — in 35 minutes

One way			Round trip		
£	s.	d.	£	s.	d.
15	0	0	30	0	0
19	0	0	38	0	0
23	0	0	46	0	0
27	0	0	54	0	0
5	0	0	10	0	0
7	0	0	14	0	0
2	10	0	5	0	0
1	5	0	2	10	0
2	0	0	4	0	0
3	15	0	7	10	0
1	17	6	3	15	0
4	4	0	8	8	0

Above: Tamanrasset with the Rootes group Humber Super Snipe on desert trials.

Opposite top: A motorised ramp being used to load a Buick at Lympne.

Opposite bottom: 1952 Timetable and Fares List showing the new Southampton–Cherbourg and Lympne–Southend routes.

A model of the proposed Blackburn Universal Freighter car ferry project.

Bristol 170 Mk 32 'Superfreighter' G-AMWA in Silver City delivery colours (1953).

CHAPTER 5

SMOKING OR *NICHT RAUCHEN*

The strategy for 1953 was to attack the mass market – that is the family car owner – and with this in mind, the fares were reduced yet again. They were now between £7 10s 0d and £20 0s 0d for cars, depending on length; while passengers were £2 0s 0d and bicycles just 5s 0d. The fares were now split into six categories. The attractions of the Air Ferry were emphasised in its advertisements as being speed, novelty, minimum handling, general convenience and personal service. Another plus was that the Foreign Currency Allowance had been raised to £40 0s 0d (equivalent to about £840 today).

The bold move of cutting fares was based on the expectation that lower fares equalled more traffic and therefore better revenue load factors. The 'ace in the hole' was the belief that the Superfreighter with only a 15 per cent higher operating cost would carry up to 50 per cent more payload per trip. All these things happened; in fact, from the traffic point of view, 'the roof came off'. On some days, more than sixty round trips a day were achieved on the Lympne-Le Touquet route.

At this time, Silver City was still operating on the Berlin-Hamburg Airlift. On 19 January 1953, Bristol 170 G-AICM left Berlin for the flight to Hamburg with Captain Dave Flett as the pilot and a radio operator as the second crew member. (Dave Flett was to become the Silver City chief pilot in later years and he will reappear later in the story.) As they neared Hamburg the weather clamped in and it was decided to return to Berlin – only to find that it was closed and would not be reopened for them even though the aircraft was now seriously short of fuel. The only choice left was to crash land – at night and in poor visibility. Dave Flett gingerly put the aircraft down in what he thought was a flat-looking area and luckily – after a great deal of lurching and bumping – came to a halt with neither of the crew suffering any injury.

As Dave looked out of the cockpit-side window he could see a light coming towards him and growing larger all the time. But what was it? Suddenly the light turned into a stream of lights and passed him with a 'whoosh'. The object was a German express train that had hurtled past only feet away from him. The aircraft had come to rest on the main railway line to Hamburg; luckily two tracks were still clear. Dave climbed out and sat on

the wing trying to recover his nerves. He took out a cigarette and lit it. '*Nicht rauchen!*
Nicht rauchen!' ('No smoking!') screamed a woman. 'Don't worry Madam,' Dave said,
'There aren't even any fumes left in it!' The aircraft was a write-off.

In February, Silver City began a contract for the Libyan Government which required
them to set up and operate an air service between its twin capitals of Tripoli and Benghazi.
Two 170s were painted in Libyan Airways livery and alterations were made to their holds
so that they could accommodate a mixture of goats, sheep, camels, horses and people in
various combinations and numbers. The aircraft then left for Libya where they operated
a daily service. Transporting your camel would cost you the princely sum of £24 0s 0d.

March saw more companies acquired by British Aviation Services. One of them was
Aquila Airways – a Southampton-based flying boat company with routes to Madeira,
the Canary Islands and Lisbon. They flew Short Sandringhams and Solent-class flying
boats which they also used in the Berlin Airlift – alighting on the large Lake Havel.
Later, another company to come under the British Aviation Services umbrella was Air
Kruise. This was a small company also operating out of Lympne and owned by Wing
Commander Hugh Kennard and his wife Audrey. They operated de Havilland Dragon
Rapide aircraft on both charter and pleasure flights, as well as a scheduled service to Le
Touquet. They were to be the forerunner of the Silver City Passenger Division.

In April the company took delivery of two ex-RAF Dakotas registered to them
as G-AMYV and G-AMYX. They were used to operate scheduled services to Basle,
Ostend, Zurich and Le Touquet together with some charter work. The first two of
the new Superfreighters (G-AMWA and G-AMWB) were also put into service at the
beginning of April 1953. With their arrival, the company was able to sell duty-free goods
in the enlarged passenger cabin; the smokers had a field day with their packs of 200
'ciggies'. These sales alone made a handsome profit of £30,000 in the first year.

In May 1953 another route was added to the network – Gatwick to Le Touquet. At
this time, Gatwick was only a small local airport with aircraft still using the original round
'Beehive' terminal building and control tower. There was also a railway station right
alongside the airport with direct services to London. On this route, passengers could get
from central London to the beach at Le Touquet in 105 minutes. The service was operated
on a twice-daily schedule; the fare being just £4 0s 0d. On 6 May, one of the Superfreighters
(G-AMWA) made a demonstration flight from Birmingham to Le Touquet, sponsored by
the AA. The aircraft carried a load of two cars, two motorcycles and twenty passengers.
However, the route was not taken up commercially until two years later.

Also in May, the Britavia part of the business provided Silver City pilots to English
Electric to deliver their Canberra jet bombers to foreign air forces. On one of these
flights, Silver City Captain 'Johnnie' Hackett and his navigation officer Rob Damon set
a new East to West trans-Atlantic speed record on the delivery flight to the Venezuelan
Air Force. These jet pilots had deliberately been employed on the Air Ferry for just such
a ferrying job. 'Taffy' had struck gold again! Meanwhile, two more Superfreighters had
joined the fleet: G-AMWC and G-AMWD.

During June, the Berlin Airlift was still going strong and was threatening to absorb
some of the 170s needed to cope with the record-breaking levels of traffic being

experienced on the Air Ferry. In a brilliant coup, Silver City managed to lease a Breguet Br761S, known as a 'Deux Ponts', from the French manufacturers. This was the second of three pre-production aircraft and was flown from Toulouse to Berlin by Silver City's Captain C.I. 'Hoppy' Hopkins in the same month.

The Br761 was a huge aircraft with four Pratt & Whitney radial engines, a wingspan of 141ft and two cargo decks and could lift 13 tons of freight. According to a report in *Flight* magazine for 16 October 1953, the aircraft (which remained on the French register as F-BASL) completed 240 hours flying and 127 round trips between Berlin and Hamburg under 'Hoppy' Hopkins' command during its three-month lease to Silver City. Towards the end of this period, the Breguet was carrying 170,000lb of freight in six round trips per day – loaded on the outward journey to Hamburg and empty on the return to Berlin. The total cargo carried amounted to nearly 4 million lb. The Breguet was also faster than the Bristol Freighter and was able to do the work of 3.25 of the smaller aircraft. As a result, three Freighters could be released for Air Ferry duties back at Lympne. Because of its performance in Germany, the 'Deux Ponts' design was considered for the Air Ferry (where it could have carried six cars – three on each of its two decks) but this idea was not taken up – indeed only about twenty of the aircraft were built.

The company's Head Office was extremely busy with all this activity going on and Taffy himself was a very busy man. His patience sometimes wore a bit thin and he didn't suffer fools or failures gladly. Most managers were threatened with dismissal on a fairly regular basis and this was accepted as 'the norm'. On a bad day, Taffy felt the need to pick up his phone and hurl it across the room where it hit the wall and disintegrated with a great crash. This was not a 'one-off' occurrence and in those days the sets were owned by Post Office Telephones, who actually showed Taffy the 'yellow card' by telling him that unless the casualty rate declined he wouldn't get any more phones.

In July 1953, another licence was granted – for the unbelievably short route from Southampton to Bembridge (Isle of Wight). The fare was to be between £3 2s 6d and £6 17s 0d, once again dependent on the length of the vehicle. Captain George Hogarth, the Eastleigh chief pilot, flew the inaugural flight on 2 July with a cargo of twelve passengers, two cars and a scooter. However, the service was not proceeded with due to problems with the airfield at Bembridge.

By the end of July, with the arrival of the last two Superfreighters (G-AMWE and G-AMWF), all six of the Superfreighters had been delivered to add to the fleet of Mk 21s. Imagine the crowded scene on the small airfield at Lympne. When it rained hard the grass really got churned up and on many occasions the aircraft had to be pulled out of the mud by a tractor. Something had to be done. The airfield was not a suitable site for expansion and so the only option was to move – but where? In typical Taffy fashion it was decided that if existing airfields were unsuitable then the answer was to build a new one.

Accordingly, Eoin Mekie – the chairman of the Silver City Airways board – persuaded the giant shipping company P&O to inject a considerable amount of cash into the company for expansion. They recruited Mr John Alcock (the younger brother of Sir John Alcock, famous for his 1919 trans-Atlantic flight in a Vickers Vimy with Sir Arthur

Whitten Brown) to find a suitable site on which to build the new airport. After reviewing Alcock's fairly small list of possible sites that met their criteria it was decided that the best site was near to the town of Lydd at the northern end of Dungeness point on the Kent coast. A contract was awarded to Richard Costain at a price of £400,000 (about £8.4 million today) and the airport was to be ready for use in the following summer – a tall order.

The year ended with a staggering increase over the previous year's figures:

       21,700 cars carried;

       8,200 motorcycles carried;

       6,600 pedal cycles carried; and

       91,000 passengers carried – an increase of about a third on 1952.

6. Jahr - Nr. 16   BERLIN - DIENSTAG - 20. JANUAR 1953   15 Pf. - Ausw. 20 Pf.

DER TAG

UNABHÄNGIGE ZEITUNG FÜR DEUTSCHLAND

Bruchlandung, aber niemand kam ums Leben: Ein britisches Flugzeug ging wegen Benzinmangels auf S-Bahn-Gleise nieder. Bericht siehe Seite 3. (Foto: AP)

Die Notlandung auf dem S-Bahn-Gelände

Newspaper headlines of the G-AICM crash in Berlin.

Berlin, 19. 1. (Eigenbericht). Amerikanische onteure des Flugplatzes Tempelhof waren m gesamten Montag nachmittag damit be- häftigt. Teile der auf dem Bahngelände | Während der ganzen Zeit stand die Flug- platz-Zentrale funktelegrafisch mit der Ma- schine in Verbindung, und auch auf dem Radarschirm zeichnete sich ihr Bild ab. Bis es | bog die Schiene einer S-Bahnstrecke über 15 Zentimeter zur Seite. Die Hauptbeschädi- gungen erlitt die Maschine am Mittelteil des Lagerraumes, wo in der Hauptsache Stoffe auf-

Above: February 1953 with one of the Silver City Bristol 170s in Libyan Airways livery being loaded with a two-year-old Friesian cow and four fourteen-day-old Friesian calves on the Tripoli-Benghazi contract.

Below: Two of Aquila Airways' Short Solent flying boats moored off Hamble in August 1955.

Right: An Air Kruise de Havilland Dragon Rapide at Lympne.

Below: A Bristol 170 Mk 32 with three export Austin A30s outside the 'Beehive' terminal at the old Gatwick Airport in 1953.

The Gatwick to Le Touquet summer 1953 fares brochure.

A picture of the May 1953 AA demonstration flight was used on the cover of this members' questionnaire to ask if the route would be attractive to them.

A Silver City DC3 on the Berlin Airlift.

The Breguet Br761S 'Deux Ponts' in Silver City livery in 1953.

Smoking or Nicht Rauchen

FERRYFIELD
AIRPORT LYDD KENT

DESIGNED AND
CONSTRUCTED
BY
RICHARD COSTAIN LTD
IN
SIX MONTHS
FOR
SILVER CITY AIRWAYS LIMITED
LONDON W.1.

BUILDING & CIVIL ENGINEERING CONTRACTORS
111, WESTMINSTER BRIDGE ROAD, LONDON, S.E.1.
WATERLOO 4977

MIDDLE EAST RHODESIA NIGERIA CANADA

Above: The Richard Costain advertisement for the construction of Ferryfield (Lydd).

Opposite top: The Isle of Wight fares brochure for 1953.

Opposite bottom: Lympne became very crowded with the introduction of the Mk 32 Superfreighter.

CHAPTER 6

A NEW HOME

1954 was to be a landmark year for Silver City with the anticipated opening of their purpose-built airport at Lydd but there were many other events taking place before that day arrived. In January, the company opened what was to be a short-lived winter sports service for skiers from Blackbushe to Zurich; the noisy 3½-hour flight was not easy to enjoy! The service was planned to operate until March – which it did – but it did not appear again.

While we are in a chilly frame of mind it is appropriate to mention that the heating system even in the new Superfreighters was pretty basic. The source of the heat was a 'Janitrol' heater installed in the starboard forward section of the hold. It was essentially a controlled blow-lamp creating hot air – and, yes, it ran on petrol, with the exhaust going overboard in the same nose area. A good indication that the heater was working was the black streak of soot down the fuselage side. Reliability was also a dubious point and experienced winter travellers wore thick coats. What would 'Health & Safety' make of it today?!

With the injection of cash by P&O came a change of ownership. In February 1954, General Steam Navigation (a subsidiary of P&O) took control of British Aviation Services and Britavia, together with their subsidiaries – including both Silver City and Aquila. The Berlin Airlift had finally come to an end and released the aircraft involved, which meant that a 170 fleet of five Mk 21s and six Superfreighters was now available. During these early months, the Mk 21s were converted to passenger trim providing seats for the Ostend schedule and charter flights.

The Britavia board, with its links to shipping lines, now looked at the merits of going into the long-range trooping market and decided to buy six Handley Page Hermes aircraft from BOAC. The Hermes had four Bristol Hercules engines, each developing over 2,100hp. It could carry eighty-eight passengers in a pressurised cabin at a cruising altitude of 24,000ft and a speed of 300mph. The first aircraft was delivered to Blackbushe in Britavia livery in May 1954 with the rest following over a two-month period. The trooping flights to Malta, Egypt, Cyprus and Singapore began in July.

In the previous chapter it was mentioned that the big Breguet aircraft used on the Berlin Airlift was considered as a possible replacement for the 170s. Now it was being considered again – this time to operate an Air Ferry service between Gatwick and Cormeilles, north-west of Paris, carrying eight cars and forty passengers – but nothing more came of it.

It was hoped that Silver City's new base at Ferryfield (Lydd) would be operational in the spring of 1954 but delays in the construction of the runways prevented this and Lympne had to soldier on operating all flights. It was decided to separate the intended Lydd flights by setting up a completely independent facility at Lympne in a marquee clearly marked 'Lydd'. (Those readers having difficulty in separating 'Lympne' from 'Lydd' are not alone; many people for a long time thought they were the same place being mispronounced.) The scheme was very successful in spite of the pilots trying to blow the marquee away with their propeller wash!

In June it was clear that Lydd was only weeks away from completion and late in that month one of the 170s made several passes and landings to try it out. A week later, 'Taffy' Powell flew into Lydd to watch a new Superfreighter G-ANWG – just days old from the factory – perform taxying tests under the command of Captain Len Madelaine (the then chief pilot) with his co-pilot Captain Dave Flett. The aircraft was part of an order that had been placed for a further three Superfreighters and G-ANWH and G-ANWI would arrive later in the month, bringing the Superfreighter fleet to nine. June had seen the start of a new route from Lympne to Calais Marck Airport and this service continued to operate from Lympne until the autumn.

12 July saw frantic activity at Lympne; everything that had to be moved down to Lydd for the next day's opening had to be prepared after that day's flying had finished. The material was flown or driven by road to Lydd. At last the great day had arrived and at eight o'clock on the morning of 13 July 1954, the inaugural flight took off for Le Touquet with local dignitaries on board. The airport had been very aptly named 'Ferryfield' (so no more Lydd to confuse with Lympne). During that day many senior staff from various branches of the group came to see 'the new baby'. Meanwhile, business continued of course and nearly seventy flights were made that day.

The new airport had two tarmac-covered concrete runways in a criss-cross pattern; one nearly 3,600ft in length in a north-east–south-west direction and a shorter one 3,000ft long in a north-west–south-east direction. Both were 120ft wide with lighting for night operations. The 300ft-long terminal building and control tower complex was situated to the north of the south-western end of the main runway and was fronted by an extensive apron long enough to accommodate six Superfreighters parked wing tip to wing tip. Tie-down shackle points were built into the apron so that the aircraft could be restrained if severe winds were forecast. There were several parking bays for aircraft waiting to be brought into service, cleaned or maintained, towards the north-western end of the shorter runway.

Facilities housed in the terminal complex included check-in desks, the departure lounge, Customs and Immigration, baggage handling, AA and RAC offices, a branch of Lloyds Bank, a snack bar, shop and a large licensed restaurant. The aircrew room and flight despatch were under the two-storey part of the building on which the control tower was sited. The freight sheds were situated at the western end of the apron, with the fire, ambulance, refuellers and engineering crew room being at the eastern end. The whole building was modern, light and airy. Waiting passengers could watch the apron activities from the glass-fronted departure lounge or the restaurant. Another key factor was the company's employment of its own Air Traffic Control staff who could operate the new Decca 4-2-4 Airfield Control Radar which enabled them, in conjunction with their Le Touquet counterparts, to watch the aircraft outbound at 1,000ft and inbound at 2,000ft.

When the airfield was built a new access road was needed to link the airfield with the existing B2075 road. A petrol filling station was also built to be run by Shell. Adjacent to this were the underground tanks where the bowsers used to fill up with aviation fuel. Just before this filling station was a sharp left bend in the narrow road and then a small bridge crossing one of the many dykes, which had to be crossed with respect. In addition to the airport's licensed bar there was also the 'Wingspan Social Club' for Silver City staff which became a popular place to spend an hour or so after work. When it was time to go home 'after a few', that narrow bridge became a severe hazard and the large Romney Marsh frogs quite often had unexpected visitors! The airport's registered owner was Ferry Airports, another Britavia company.

In August, Taffy scored another first when a leased Westland-Sikorsky S51 'Dragonfly' helicopter complete with Silver City markings arrived at Ferryfield to open a trial service to Le Touquet. The main purpose of the trial was to test one of Taffy's latest ideas which was to replace the conventional aircraft used on the Channel crossings with huge twin-rotor 'aerial-crane'-type helicopters which could drop down onto large containers loaded with – well, almost anything. The Dragonfly trial proved what he had suspected – that helicopters were very expensive to operate and not as reliable as fixed wing aircraft – so another idea bit the dust.

It was a sad day on 3 October when 'Mac' McRae hauled down the Silver City flag at Lympne for the last time as the final flight departed with the Silver City chairman Eoin Mekie on board. Lympne had served Silver City well since 1948 with nearly 55,000 vehicles and 208,500 passengers carried – all without incident. At the end of 1954, Silver City still had their sights set on route expansion for the coming year and had applied for a licence to operate an Air Ferry service from Stranraer in Scotland to Belfast in Northern Ireland.

During one day in July there were 222 crossings of the English Channel by Silver City aircraft; crews often flying six round trips a day. The accuracy of the course flown from one airport to the other was very important both in flight times and fuel economy, so Silver City fitted a Decca Navigation system to their aircraft to work with the equipment installed in the control tower. This took the form of a rolling map display which enabled the pilots to fly the route to the accuracy required.

As might be expected, some pretty dramatic traffic figures emerged at the end of 1954. They were:

> 30,976 cars carried;
> 11,541 motor and pedal cycles carried; and
> 112,000 passengers carried.

Above: Bristol 170 Mk 32 G-AMWA at Ferryfield in 1960. The picture shows Silver City engineer Les Dray attending to its starboard engine; the aircraft's heater exhaust is clearly visible below the aircraft's name.

Below: A rare picture of Britavia Hermes G–ALDU at Blackbushe.

A view of Calais Marck check–in.

Ferryfield, operational in 1954, viewed from overhead the threshold of runway 04; six Bristol 170 Mk 32s, one Mk 21, a DC3 and an Airspeed Consul can be seen. The Passenger Division buildings are yet to be built.

The terminal building showing the check-in desks.

Ferryfield on 27 August 1954 with Westland-Sikorsky S51 Dragonfly helicopter G-ANLV. The Air Operating Certificate had just been handed over for Silver City to operate a helicopter on the cross-Channel route.

Above: An Air Charter Bristol 170 Mk 32.

Left: 'Mac' McRae (left) at Lympne holding the Silver City flag that he had just lowered for the last time on 3 October 1954. On the right are Lew Turner and Silver City chairman Eoin Mekie.

A Highland regiment boards a Britavia Handley Page Hermes at Blackbushe in 1954.

Overhead Ferryfield looking westwards.

The Ferryfield Fire Section with vintage engines NOU 668 and HUC 799. The latter is an ex-RAF Fordson WOT 1 Foam Tender dating from 1942 and is now preserved in the RAF Manston Spitfire & Hurricane Memorial Museum.

The cockpit of a Bristol 170 Mk 21.

CHAPTER 7

SCOTCH AND SHAMROCKS

1955 arrived and once again fares were reduced. One of the first notable events was the grant of a new licence to operate an Air Ferry route between Stranraer and Belfast. The airfields chosen were Castle Kennedy and Newtownards; the journey time was twenty minutes – approximately the same as Ferryfield to Le Touquet. The family-sized car fare was £7 0s 0d (equivalent to about £140 today) and the inaugural flight took place on 7 April. The day before this event, Silver City opened a fifty-minute Air Ferry route from Southampton to Deauville (Saint Gatien). This route was to be operated during the summer season on a twice-daily basis. Also in April, Air Kruise moved their operations from Lympne to Ferryfield and acquired two more Dakotas. With this increase in fleet size they were able to operate charter flights to a large number of European destinations. They also began inclusive tour flights for such up-and-coming pioneers in this field as Lewis Leroy of Tunbridge Wells. Eventually, 'No Passport' trips to France were to follow. In need of more modern aircraft, Air Kruise placed a provisional order for six of the new Handley Page Herald passenger aircraft but these options were never taken up. In June an 'on demand' Air Ferry and freight service was offered from Liverpool (Woodvale) to Belfast.

Silver City now employed forty-two pilots at Ferryfield and six at Southampton, one of whom was Jerry Rosser who had been on the inaugural flight from Lympne back in 1948. He had now amassed 5,500 Channel crossings!! The Birmingham to Le Touquet Air Ferry service started on 17 June with a flight time of eighty-five minutes. This route was to end in the autumn. August saw Captain Hackett and Navigator Moneypenny in an English Electric Canberra bomber, this time establishing a new record by crossing the Atlantic and back in the same day. 'Taffy' was perfectly aware of the publicity value of these events and made sure that the Press knew which company provided the crew.

The company's first serious incident occurred on 9 August when a Bristol 170, having just taken off from Calais, suffered a double engine failure for no obvious reason. The captain managed to vault the canal and brought the aircraft to rest in a field; nobody was hurt and only the undercarriage and tail of the aircraft suffered any damage – a lucky escape.

November provided a number of milestone events for the company; on the 4th, Taffy Powell was presented with the coveted Cumberbatch Trophy by His Royal Highness the

Duke of Edinburgh. The trophy is awarded by the Guild of Air Pilots and Air Navigators (GAPAN) to the company with the best air safety record in the previous year. Britavia weighed-in on 14 November when one of their Hermes aircraft operated a charter flight for ships' crews from Blackbushe through Shannon and Gander to New York. This was the first time that a Hermes had ever made a trans-Atlantic flight.

Taffy and the board were once again looking for replacement aircraft, particularly with a view to operating longer-range Air Ferry routes deep into Europe. A number of aircraft manufacturers were asked to submit designs, among them was Armstrong Whitworth – makers of the RAF's twin-boom Argosy freighters. They proposed a 'flattened' version designated the A.W.670 that could have accommodated six cars in two rows side by side. Handley Page also submitted a design based broadly on their Herald. During the year Silver City became the largest carrier of air freight in the country with 70,190 tons.

Like anything that proves a great success, sooner or later someone else will want to emulate it. In April 1955 that 'someone' was the then unknown Freddie Laker who had an aviation engineering company based at Southend. He bought some 170s from Bristols and opened his own Air Ferry services between Southend and Calais and Southend and Ostend. His company was 'Air Charter', later to become 'Channel Air Bridge', but that's another story.

There are many groups of people whose efforts played a big part in the Silver City success story and one group whose world was just about to broaden quite dramatically were the engineers. During the early years, all the heavy maintenance on the Bristol 170s was done by British Aviation Services at their Blackbushe base, while the day-to-day minor maintenance and 'running repairs' were handled by the Silver City staff on site at Lympne. With the move to Ferryfield this quickly changed. The engineering workload had risen steeply with the increased number of aircraft requiring maintenance. Before too long, there would be of a fleet of twenty 170s and six Dakotas, all requiring some form of maintenance.

The first step was the construction of a big hangar, visible for miles across the flat Romney Marsh and a heaven-sent haven for most of the birds in the area. The hangar was large enough to house three Superfreighters nose to tail and was completed at the end of 1955. Supporting workshops adjoined the hangar to provide an Engine Overhaul Bay; Instrument, Electrical, and Radio Workshops; Detail Metal Repair Shop; Flying Surface Repair Shop; Upholstery Repair Shop; and a huge Store housing the spares. All these were on the ground floor. On a small mezzanine floor were some of the administration offices, spares control, technical records and a vital link – the planning department. Here a small staff produced the maintenance programmes for this large fleet of aircraft – all with pens and pencils – no computers in those days! A comprehensive Motor Transport department looked after the company's vehicles.

The engineering task had two main aspects. One was to carry out the heavy maintenance programmes in the winter when several aircraft could be in for many weeks of major checks requiring them to be completely stripped down. In later years the 170s suffered problems with the main spar due to the continuous sequence of take-offs and landings; the fix was to take the wings off, remove the centre section and pack it all off to Bristols for repair. There was, therefore, on occasions a fuselage as well as the three aircraft in the hangar, quite a squeeze.

Most of the staff were engaged on this heavy work during the winter, with a small group covering the requirements of the aircraft out on service. In the summer, the situation was completely reversed. The majority of the hangar engineers started a three-shift system and went onto 'The Line' (as it was known) to put as much manpower as possible in place to deal with whatever problems the operating aircraft threw at them. This might even be an engine change. Meanwhile, those left in the hangar carried out the short duration checks that all the aircraft needed. At Ferryfield, there was no going home at five o'clock; the fleet had to be ready for business the next day. Aircraft cleaning bays running the length of the side of the hangar made sure that the aircraft were spick and span.

Talking of technical matters, the Bristol 170 had a tail wheel which 'castored', allowing the tail to turn when taxying. This tail wheel had to be locked centrally when the aircraft was taking off or landing. It was controlled by a switch in the cockpit which electrically operated a pin in the tail wheel mounting. It was not unknown for this pin to get stuck in the 'IN' position on landing – in spite of the crew switching it to 'OUT'. With the pin 'IN' it was difficult to turn the aircraft and this resulted in the tail wheel tyre being scuffed to pieces – a process that was accompanied by loud squealing noises. To the surprise of the passengers, the co-pilot would appear from the hold door brandishing a crash axe. He would then open the main cabin door and vanish for a few moments before coming back in and retracing his steps to the cockpit. A well-aimed blow would usually release the pin, whereupon the aircraft would resume its taxying. On one occasion, however, while this 'adjustment' was being made, the captain thought his co-pilot was back on board and proceeded to taxy back to the terminal leaving his crew member stranded on the runway with the axe – and a mile to walk home!

There are many other humorous tales to tell. One of these goes back to 1954 and concerns a student nurse who, at the tender age of twenty, met a solicitor with a lovely new Alvis sports car. After a week or so, he asked her if she would like to go on a rally with him to France. She said yes – but upon seeking permission from her rather 'Victorian' father got a resounding 'NO'. Shortly after this she asked him if she could go to Torquay – no mention of the boyfriend. Grudgingly he agreed and she set about arranging for postcards to be sent from Torquay and then set off for Ferryfield where she and the boyfriend took the Silver City flight, complete with the Alvis, to Le Touquet. After they had disembarked, the Alvis took the eye of a journalist writing an article for *Motor* magazine. He asked if he could take a picture of the car and, to add a touch of glamour, could the young lady perch on the bonnet? 'OK,' said the boyfriend. Two weeks later, the young nurse arrived home to an electric atmosphere; her parents quickly produced a copy of the *Evening Standard* bearing a large picture of their daughter on the Alvis. The caption read: 'Twenty minutes ago she was in Kent.' Eventually she was forgiven after her parents received a further eleven copies of the paper from relatives saying how proud they must be of her!

1955 ended on a high note with increases in traffic in the order of 30 per cent over the 1954 figures. The year's totals were:

42,589 cars carried; and
160,219 passengers carried.

SILVER CITY

NORTHERN IRELAND

AIR FERRY

for cars, cycles and passengers

BELFAST · STRANRAER
1956

AIR FERRY TIME TABLE 1956

(Flying time: 17 minutes)

SUMMER SCHEDULES

Daily from 30th April until 14th October, 1956 (both dates inclusive)

Belfast (Newtownards)	*Dep.* 09.30	12.30	15.30	17.00
Stranraer (Castle Kennedy)	*Dep.* 10.05	13.05	16.05	17.35

Supplementary Services will be operated when required

WINTER SCHEDULES

Daily from 1st January until 29th April and from 15th October to 31st December, 1956 (all dates inclusive)

Belfast (Newtownards)	*Dep.* 10.00	12.00	14.00
Stranraer (Castle Kennedy)	*Dep.* 11.00	13.00	15.00

Extra Services will be operated over Easter

Passengers should check in at the airport 30 minutes before the advertised departure time of their flight.

THE CROSS-CHANNEL AIR FERRY

Silver City operates frequent Air Ferry services every day throughout the year from Lydd (Ferryfield) Airport, in Kent, to Le Touquet, and commencing in February this year a new ferry service from Southampton to Guernsey. Full details of all Silver City services are obtainable from Silver City Airways Ltd., 11 Great Cumberland Place, London, W.1, or from any Silver City office or agent.

FREIGHT   Silver City operates daily freight services to and from the Continent, between Stranraer and Belfast, and between Southampton and Guernsey. Details of these can be obtained from Silver City Airways Ltd., 11 Gt. Cumberland Place, London, W.1 (Tel.: PADdington 7040), or Newtownards Airport, Newtownards, Co. Down (Tel. Newtownards: 2320 and 2324).

Above: The new Belfast to Stranraer Air Ferry service brochure.

Opposite: Captain Jerry Rosser at the controls of a Handley Page Herald.

The record-breaking English Electric Canberra bomber that completed the London–New York–London round trip in the same day (14 hours, 21 minutes and 45.4 seconds). It covered 6,916 miles.

Silver City's crew of 'Johnnie' Hackett and Peter Moneypenny leave their Canberra bomber at Heathrow on 24 August 1955.

An artist's impression of the proposed A.W.670.

An artist's impression of the A.W.670 in 'Air Ferry' service.

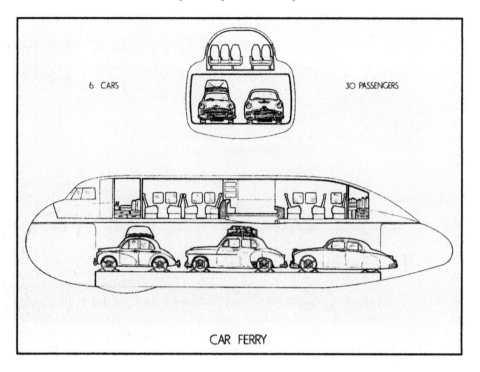

Schematic of the A.W.670 in its 'Air Ferry' configuration.

The hangar floor at Ferryfield, marked out to represent the A.W.670 hold area; staff cars are used to simulate the load.

The new hangar almost completed. It could house three Bristol 170 Mk 32s.

Bristol 170 G-ANWM undergoing a major check, whilst in the background another Mk 32 has had its wings removed for main spar modifications.

A Bristol 170 Mk 32 on a major check in the hangar at Ferryfield.

Bristol 170 Mk 32 G-ANWK on a major check. Inspector/Chargehand Jack Hayman and Engineering Manager Brian Sparrow discuss a technical matter.

This page: The Powerplant Bay at Ferryfield.

Above: An unusual air-to-air picture of two Bristol 170s.

Opposite top: A picture of a Bristol 170 Mk 32 showing the short distance between the main cabin door and the tail wheel.

Opposite bottom: The Air Kruise fleet continued to grow – a rare picture of four Dakotas at Ferryfield.

CHAPTER 8

ROYAL APPROVAL

In 1956 Silver City raised their fares for the first time and, not surprisingly, the traffic figures dropped back a little by the end of the year. On 22 March, Silver City's tentacles reached out to the Channel Islands when an Air Ferry service started from Southampton to Guernsey (La Villaize) Airport; hundreds of boxes of flowers made up the return cargo. By the end of the year, 100,000 boxes had been brought to England in this way. A similar service to Jersey was introduced on 1 July.

In May, after dabbling in the London–Paris road-air market, the company decided to open a coach-air service between those two capitals and another between London and Brussels. The East Kent Road Car Co. provided forty-four-seat luxury coaches to take passengers from London to Ferryfield, from where a 170 Mk 21 configured for the same number of passengers flew them to Le Touquet. The passengers then boarded a smart newly built 'Auto-Rail' coach at Etaples railway station; the train then whisked the passengers off to the Gare du Nord terminal in Paris. The service was known as the Silver Arrow and departed from London at eight o'clock in the morning and again at two o'clock in the afternoon. Similarly, there were two departures from Paris for the return journey. The single fare was £8 0s 0d and the journey time was seven hours.

The highpoint of 1956 came on 5 April when His Royal Highness the Duke of Edinburgh paid a visit to Ferryfield. He arrived at eleven o'clock in a de Havilland Heron of the Queen's Flight and was greeted by Eoin Mekie, the Silver City chairman, and 'Taffy' Powell, the managing director. His Royal Highness was taken on a conducted tour of the airport which included a visit to the hangar: all the engineering staff were lined up resplendent in spotless new overalls – on which the Duke commented with a wry smile. When the tour was over, Taffy and the Duke's party were escorted across the apron to waiting Superfreighter G-AMWD. This aircraft was loaded with two new sports cars – a Sunbeam Rapier and a Triumph TR3. The flight was commanded by Captain Dave Flett and his co-pilot was Captain 'Hoppy' Hopkins. The steward cum car marshal was Mike Liddiard.

Dave Flett wound the nose doors shut with the wheel on the side of the hold and then, knowing that the Duke liked to participate, asked him if he would like to lock the mechanical door latches that held the edges of the doors securely closed; the Duke happily did so. What neither of them knew was that in an attempt to make everything smarter than smart, Engineering had applied a fresh coat of red paint to the latches the night before. All was revealed when the Duke stood there with red blotchy hands. Staff were despatched at high speed to the nearest source of paint cleaner and the Duke was soon restored to pristine condition. The two pilots and the Duke climbed up the crew ladder and into the cockpit. The Duke, a pilot himself, took the controls and flew the aircraft to within a few miles of Le Touquet where he handed over to Dave Flett because there was a strong crosswind at the airport.

On arrival, the Duke was greeted by an Honour Guard of the Gendarmerie Nationale lined up for his inspection, their commander magnificent in his gold-bedecked uniform. When the inspection was over, the officer saluted smartly, whereupon the Duke beckoned him forward and raised his lapel. The commander stiffened with pride and grew six inches; what decoration was he going to receive? The Duke put his hand in his pocket and produced a small round red and white tin button badge inscribed 'We fly Silver City' which he pinned on to the commander's lapel. The commander took it in good spirit among the stifled chortles from the onlookers – Taffy being one of them. After an excellent lunch the Duke departed in his Heron.

Later in May, Manx Airlines – based in the Isle of Man – was taken over by British Aviation Services. This company operated charter and freight services from the north of England with de Havilland Dragon Rapides and Dakotas. Their two Dakotas were to be transferred to Air Kruise and replaced with two Bristol 170 Mk 21s from Silver City.

Another royal personage to pass through Ferryfield was King Feisal of Iraq who, on 12 August, flew out on a Superfreighter at the end of his State Visit. During November 1956 a total of twenty-six round trips were flown to Vienna taking medical supplies and blankets to refugees from the Hungarian Uprising and bringing many of those displaced people back to Britain. Silver City operated the relief campaign using three Dakotas borrowed from Air Kruise. A new passenger terminal opened at Ferryfield for Air Kruise and this was capable of handling 2,000 passengers a day. It was a valuable addition with the increase in Air Kruise business.

Other notable events in the year were the delivery of five more new Superfreighters – G-ANWJ through to G-ANWN – bringing the Superfreighter fleet to fourteen. This enabled three of the smaller passenger-configured Mk 21s to be transferred to Air Kruise where they were desperately needed. The holds of these passenger-configured aircraft had been trimmed to take away the bare metal look but the seats were more like bus seats and were not very comfortable on a long flight. In October, one of the largest loads carried to date was flown by a Superfreighter from Blackbushe to Greenland; it was a 'Dragonfly' helicopter owned by Autair of Luton.

An excursion into the world of entertainment occurred when Silver City provided a Mk 21 to perform in the film *The Man in the Sky* which was being filmed at Wolverhampton Airport and starred Jack Hawkins. The film company asked if during a landing shot the pilot could 'wiggle it about a bit' as if he was in trouble. This he did – but after touch-down, on the landing roll out, the notoriously poor brakes on the Mk 21 decided to have a day off and the aircraft ran off into a ditch – much to the delight of the film crew. They certainly got their money's worth that day.

In December, the Lancashire Aircraft Corporation became another British Aviation Services acquisition. They too operated Dakotas and de Havilland Dragon Rapides in the north of England. We shall see what all these acquisitions in the north led to in the next chapter.

During the summer of 1956 the standing record of 222 crossings of the Channel in one day was broken when 246 transitions were achieved by Silver City aircraft.

Some of the East Kent coaches used on the 'Silver Arrow' Coach-Air service.

SILVER ARROW
daily rail-air service

THE Silver Arrow is a unique combination of British and French Railways' express services and Silver City's cross-Channel passenger air services.

It takes you from the centre of London to the centre of Paris in a few minutes over six hours – comfortably and inexpensively.

Fares are all-inclusive. There are no extras of any kind and seats are guaranteed throughout the journey. Refreshments are available en route.

★

From Victoria (B.R.) Station, you travel by British Railways' newly-electrified North Kent line to Margate. A coach waits to take you the short distance to Manston Airport.

The 20-minute cross-Channel flight from Manston is by Silver City's four-engined Handley Page Hermes aircraft. Duty-free cigarettes and spirits are available on board.

At Le Touquet Airport, Customs and entry formalities take only a few minutes and your journey to the Gare du Nord, Paris, is completed by French Railways' non-stop express train.

★

Passengers may join the Silver Arrow at Margate Station or Manston (served by East Kent coaches). Through passengers to Paris may arrange stop-over facilities at Le Touquet.

ECONOMY rail-air FARES

	SPRING March 1–May 28 inclusive			SUMMER May 29 onwards	
Single	Return		Single	Return
£3.12.6	£6.10.6	LONDON to LE TOUQUET	£3.13.0	£6.15.0
£4.19.0	£8.19.0	LONDON to PARIS	£5. 0.0	£9. 9.0
£3. 0.0	£6. 0.0	MANSTON to LE TOUQUET	£3. 0.0	£6. 0.0
£4.12.6	£8. 8.0	MANSTON to PARIS	£4. 6.0	£8. 1.0

CHILDREN	Aged 3 and under 10:—50% of adult fare Under 3 years of age:—10% of adult fare
	Between Manston and Le Touquet only, the 50% concession refers to children between 2 and 12. Children under 2 not occupying a seat travel free on this section.

EXCESS BAGGAGE	Free baggage allowance is 44 lbs. — thereafter charged at 5d. per lb.

DAILY TIMETABLE

May 29–October 1 inclusive

Every day				Supplementary Service from June 25-Sept. 12 inc.	
dep. 8.40 a.m.	arr. 3.05 p.m.	LONDON	dep. 2.40 p.m.	arr. 9.06 p.m.
dep. 11.05 a.m.	dep. 1.00 p.m.	MANSTON	dep. 5.10 p.m.	dep. 7.00 p.m.
dep. 12.15 p.m.	dep. 11.55 a.m.	LE TOUQUET	dep. 6.26 p.m.	dep. 6.00 p.m.
arr. 2.42 p.m.	dep. 8.42 a.m.	PARIS	arr. 9.23 p.m.	dep. 2.21 p.m.

March 1–May 28 inclusive

11.40 a.m. dep.	LONDON	arr. 6.08 p.m.
2.10 p.m. dep.	MANSTON	arr. 3.30 p.m.
2.40 p.m. arr.	LE TOUQUET	dep. 3.00 p.m.
6.11 p.m. arr.	PARIS	dep. 11.57 a.m.

NOTE: Up to and including April 9—when British Summer Time comes into force—departure times from London will be 10.40 a.m. and arrival time in London will be 5.08 p.m.

REPORTING TIMES: Passengers must report at appropriate platform in London (Victoria S.R. Station) or Paris (Gare du Nord) 15 minutes before train's scheduled departure time. If joining at Manston or Le Touquet Airports, passengers must report 30 minutes before aircraft's scheduled departure time.

There are uniformed Silver Arrow receptionists at Victoria and Margate stations to assist passengers.

The 'Silver Arrow' timetable and fares list for 1960, by which time the service was being operated by Hermes aircraft from Manston Airport.

Above: Bristol 170 Mk 32 G-AMWD ready for departure to Le Touquet. The picture shows Dave Flett, HRH the Duke of Edinburgh, Taffy Powell, Eoin Mekie and 'Hoppy' Hopkins standing in the hold. Dave Flett has the door closing wheel in his hand. The export cars can be seen behind the group.

Opposite top: His Royal Highness the Duke of Edinburgh arrives at Ferryfield in a Queen's Flight de Havilland Heron to begin his visit on 5 April 1956. Greeting him are Eoin Mekie and Taffy Powell.

Opposite bottom: The Duke talks to the Silver City engineers in the hangar.

621/1956

GENERAL DECLARATION

(OUTWARD ~~INWARDS~~)

No. 155 (Sa

Owner or Operator } SILVER CITY AIRWAYS LTD. Aircraft **G-ANWD** Flight No. **1150** Date **5.4.56**
(Registration Marks and Nationality)

Point of clearance (Place and Country) **FERRYFIELD** For entry at (Place and Country) **LE TOUQUET**

DECLARATION OF HEALTH

Illness, suspected of being of an infectious nature, which has occurred on board, during the flight **NIL.**

Any other condition on board which may lead to the spread of disease **NIL.**

Details of each disinsecting or sanitary treatment (place, date, time, method) during the flight. If no disinsecting has been carried out during the flight, give details of most recent disinsecting **NIL.**

Animals (including birds and insects) plants, unprocessed animal and plant products, cultures of bacteria, fungi and viruses, samples of soil and fertilizer on board (where required by State of arrival) **NIL.**

For official use only

H.M. CUSTOMS & EXCISE
CLEARED OUT

-5 APR 1956

Time of Departure

Time of Arrival

CREW MANIFEST

	Surname and initials	Duties on board	Nationality	Serial No. and County of Issuance of Licence or Certificate or Passport
1	FLETT D.	CAPT.	BRITISH	
2	HOPKINS C.I.	CAPT.	BRITISH	
3	LIDDIARD M.J.	SENIOR F/A.	BRITISH	
4				

PASSENGER MANIFEST (See note below)

	Surname and Initials	From	To	For use by owner or operator only	For official use only
1	HIS ROYAL HIGHNESS				
2	THE DUKE OF EDINBURGH	FER.	LET.		
3	LIEUT. COMDR. MICHAEL				
4	PARKER	"	"	2212/10642	
5	S/LDR. HENRY CHINNERY	"	"	2212/10643	
6	INSPECTOR F. KELLY	"	"	2212/10644	
7	MR. EOIN C. MEKIE	"	"	S/PASS No. 1	
8	AIR COMMODORE GRIFFITH				
9	J. POWELL	"	"	S/PASS No.11	
10	SIR WILLIAM CURRIE	"	"	2212/10645	
11	SIR DONALD ANDERSON	"	"	S/PASS No. 5	
12	MR. IAN HOOPER	"	"	S/PASS No. 14	
13	GENERAL SIR EDWIN				
14	MORRIS	"	"	S/PASS No. 3	
15	GROUP CAPT. DEANE	"	"	S/PASS No. 36	

CARGO MANIFEST (See note below)

	Marks and Numbers on packages	Number and Type of packages	Nature of Goods	From	To	Gross Weight	For use by owner or operator only
1-2	CHASSIS No. 3600605	1(ONE) CAR	SUNBEAM RAPIER	FER.	LET.	1049 Kgs.	A/CON. NOTE No. 1157 13'3"
5-6	CHASSIS No. 10152 TS	1(ONE) CAR	TRIUMPH T.R. 3	"	"	902 Kgs.	A/CON. NOTE No. 1152 12'7"

I declare, that this General Declaration all statements and particulars contained therein, and in any attached manifests or stores lists are complete and contain to the best of my knowledge and belief an exact and true account of all :-

Crew } Embarked on
Passengers } the above Aircraft
Cargo, Stores } Laden ON
Mail

Signature [signature] Pilot in command or Authorised agent

NOTE :- If separate Passenger or Cargo Manifests are used, the appropriate sections of this form should be noted " (No. of) Passenger Manifests attached " and " (No. of) Cargo Manifests attached ". The word " Nil " should be inserted across the appropriate manifest section when no passengers or cargo are carried.

The General Declaration (manifest) for the Queen's Flight.

The Guard of Honour presents arms as His Royal Highness arrives at Le Touquet.

The dignitaries pose for a picture at Le Touquet. Note the 'We fly Silver City' badge above the Commander of the Guard's medals.

The Cooper Car Co.'s 1957 Le Mans entry.

The Royal Party pause to look at Bristol 170 Mk 32 G-ANWI during the Royal Visit on 5 April 1956.

His Royal Highness the Duke of Edinburgh gazes at the wonders of the Bristol Superfreighter.

Bristol 170 Mk 21 G-AIMH wearing Silver City livery and retaining the Manx Airlines' logos.

King Feisal of Iraq at the end of his State Visit on 12 August 1956. He inspects the RAF Guard of Honour from Uxbridge with Air Vice-Marshal Cohu and Flight Lieutenant Wallace.

An Air Kruise DC3 at Linz during the Hungarian aid mission in December 1956.

The new passenger terminal built for Air Kruise at Ferryfield.

Right: The Silver City Channel Islands tariff for 1957.

Opposite top: An overhead view of a very active Ferryfield showing: fourteen Bristol 170 Mk 32s; four Bristol 170 Mk 21s; two DC3s; an Airspeed Consul; and a Decca-owned Percival Prince.

Opposite bottom: A view of the Bristol 170 Mk 21 in passenger configuration as used on the Coach-Air service.

SILVER CITY

Channel Islands Services

(Valid from March 1957)

★ ★ ★

VEHICLE AND PASSENGER FARES BETWEEN SOUTHAMPTON AND JERSEY AND GUERNSEY

Type and Overall Length of Vehicle		Single Fare
		£ s. d.
Motor Cars	Up to 12′ 9″	12 0 0
	Over 12′ 9″ to 13′ 6″ ...	14 10 0
	Over 13′ 6″ to 14′ 6″ ...	17 10 0
	Over 14′ 6″ to 15′ 6″ ...	20 0 0
	Over 15′ 6″	23 0 0
Motor Cycles	Solo, 250 c.c. or below ...	2 10 0
	Solo, over 250 c.c.	3 15 0
	Combinations	5 0 0
	Auto-cycles, Scooters ...	1 15 0
	Scooters with side-car attachments	3 10 0
	Tri-cars, etc.	7 10 0
Pedal Cycles	Ordinary	10 0
	Tandem	15 0
	Side-car, if fitted, extra to above	10 0
Caravans & Baggage Trailers	Up to 6′ 0″ overall length, including towbar	5 10 0
	Exceeding 6′ 0″—per foot ...	1 5 0
Return vehicle fares are double the single fares		

● Passengers		£ s. d.
Single		5 0 0
12-Month Return		9 0 0
Monthly Return		7 3 0 (a)
15-Day Return		5 13 0 (b)
3-Day Excursion		5 0 0 (c)

Children under two years of age travel at 10 per cent. of full fare, if not occupying a seat.

Children between two and twelve years of age travel half fare.

Caravans and trailers exceeding 6′ 6″ in height and 6′ 6″ in width cannot be accepted.

(a) Available daily except between 1st June and 14th September when the fare is not available on Saturdays

(b) Available daily except between 1st June and 5th October when this fare is restricted to Tuesday, Wednesday and Thursday only.

(c) For return flights originating in Jersey and Guernsey, available from 1st November until 31st March, and valid for three days only including day of travel.

EXCESS BAGGAGE CHARGE: Applies only to passengers travelling without vehicle—33 lbs. free, thereafter charged at 6d. per lb.

● **There is a temporary surcharge, due to increased fuel costs, of 1/- per passenger on all one-way, circle and round trip journeys between the Mainland and the Channel Islands. This is a flat surcharge of 1/- regardless of the amount of fare. There is no surcharge for inter-island journeys.**

Bristol 170 Mk 21 G-AIFV after the landing accident at Wolverhampton during the filming of *The Man in the Sky*. The film crew got more than they bargained for.

B.A.S. BUY LANCASHIRE AIRCRAFT CORPORATION
Extensive Northern Network To Operate During Coming Season

B.A.S. Group's Northern Network

Early in December it was announced that the Lancashire Aircraft Corporation had been purchased by the B.A.S. group. The airlines will continue in its own identity, based on Squires Gate Airport, Blackpool.

Together with Manx Airlines Ltd. and Silver City's Northern Ireland Air Ferry, Lancashire's services will extend and integrate our Northern network, which now holds licences as follows:—

Air Ferry.—Stranraer to Newtownards and to Ronaldsway (I.O.M.). Newtownards to Ronaldsway.

Coach/Air.—Ronaldsway to Belfast and to Glasgow.

Passenger.—Blackpool and Leeds to Ronaldsway and Jersey. Birmingham to Ronaldsway. Ronaldsway to Carlisle, Glasgow, Newcastle and Edinburgh.

AIR FERRY FARE REDUCTIONS

AT a Press conference held on Wednesday, January 2, Mr. Eoin C. Mekie, Chairman of the British Aviation Services Group, announced substantial reductions in the 1957 air ferry fares on all Continental routes.

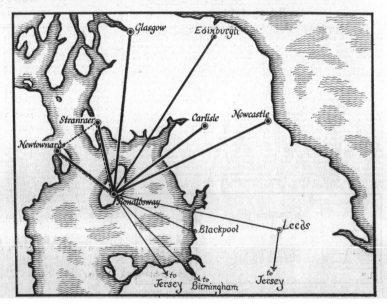

Ferry News announces the acquisition of the Lancashire Aircraft Corporation by British Aviation Services in December 1956.

Handley Page Hermes G-ALDJ undershot the runway, crashed and caught fire at Blackbushe on 6 November 1956. Ron Phillips surveys the scene.

Bristol 170 Mk 21 G-AHJD in an unusual livery. It was leased from Eagle Aviation Services during 1956 and is seen here at Lydd in 1959 with the replica Blériot monoplane in the foreground.

Bristol 170 Mk 21 G-AHJI in Air Kruise livery (1956).

Bristol 170 Mk 21 G-AGVC in Manx Airlines livery (1956).

Bristol 170 Mk 21 G–AIME airborne in 1956.

CHAPTER 9

ONE DRAGON IN; ONE DRAGON OUT

1956 had seen a significant drop in traffic compared with the previous year. Just 33,191 cars and 125,243 passengers had been carried, compared with 42,598 cars and 160,219 passengers in 1955. Silver City's reaction to this fall in traffic was to revert to their previous policy of cutting fares to attract more customers and the fares for 1957 showed a reduction of between 6 and 25 per cent. Once again, the smaller cars were the main target – the Austin A30s and Morris Minors could now travel from Ferryfield to Le Touquet for as little as £6 10s 0d (about £120 today).

Another major event was the acquisition of Dragon Airways by British Aviation Services. In common with Manx Airlines and the Lancashire Aircraft Corporation, they were operating routes in the north of England, flying twelve-seat de Havilland Herons from their base in Newcastle. These three companies now became the 'Northern Division' of Silver City Airways. Their aircraft operated in their own liveries until October 1957 when they were repainted in Silver City's livery of silver, Royal blue, and white.

Silver City now had an extensive network in the north of England with its headquarters at Blackpool's Squires Gate Airport. The company operated passenger and freight services to many destinations including Carlisle, Newcastle, Glasgow, Edinburgh, Leeds and the Isle of Man, plus some 'near-European' destinations. The maintenance for Northern Division's aircraft was carried out by Manx Engineering at Blackpool.

During the summer at Ferryfield, sixty round trips a day were commonplace; indeed it looked like a continuous stream of aircraft taking-off and landing between eight o'clock in the morning and eleven at night. At peak times, Ferryfield saw more movements than Heathrow with a take-off or landing every two minutes. To achieve this level of activity the processing of the Air Ferry passengers and their vehicles had to be well planned and executed. Here is a description of how the system worked: The passengers arrive in their car at the large car park to the rear of the terminal building where a Silver City security man looking remarkably like the infamous Mr McKay of TV's *Porridge* fame directs them to a parking space. The passengers leave their luggage in the car and walk to the terminal building. Once inside, they head for the AA or RAC counter to hand over their car's documents, then on to the ticket desk to check in. Meanwhile, their car has been collected from the car park by a Silver City driver and driven into the 'Outbound' tunnel; this passes through the terminal building and emerges onto the apron.

The tunnel has been cleverly designed with an outline of the aircraft's hold marked out on the ground where the car is standing; a height gauge is suspended from the ceiling to ensure overhead clearance once the car is loaded. Silver City know the weight of every production car made and can calculate the aircraft load and balance from their positions on the marked floor. This is the same order in which the cars will be loaded into the aircraft. While in the tunnel, the AA or RAC staff check that the car's engine and chassis numbers match with the documentation and the Customs Officers check the baggage. There is another similar tunnel for 'Inbound' traffic.

Back in the terminal, the passengers wait to be called for their flight. Only twenty-five minutes have elapsed since they arrived and in a few minutes more they are requested to go to the departure gate. Passengers are always called by name, which makes it a very personal experience, far removed from the mass treatment on the cross-Channel boats. Had they been looking out onto the apron a few minutes earlier they would have seen their car and two others being driven up the ramps and into the aircraft's hold by the Silver City drivers. Once on board, the cars are quickly shackled down and the two pilots and an air hostess in their smart navy blue uniforms can be seen making their way to the aircraft.

The first action for the aircrew is for the co-pilot to close and latch the nose doors while the captain climbs up the crew ladder into the cockpit and begins his pre-flight checks. The air hostess will be in the rear cabin stowing the duty-free goods and preparing to welcome her passengers aboard. Closing the nose doors is also the cue for the ground hostess to escort our passengers from the departure gate to the aircraft. Once on board, they will be seated and strap themselves in; the large passenger door will then be closed. While they were boarding, a David Brown or Tugmaster tractor was coupled to the aircraft's tail wheel – the reason for this is that the aircraft are always parked nose-in on the apron and stand side by side – preventing them from turning. They therefore have to be pulled back and turned through ninety degrees onto the taxiway. The tractor is uncoupled and a signal given to the pilots that the tractor is clear.

The engines are now started and the aircraft taxies to the end of the runway. It is less than forty minutes since the passengers arrived at the airport. Twenty minutes later, the wheels kiss the runway at Le Touquet and the aircraft taxies to the terminal; the passengers disembark and after a brief '*Bonjour*' to the French customs, they are reunited with their car. A few minutes more and they are motoring through the French countryside. The time elapsed since they arrived at Ferryfield is just one hour – it was *the* way to cross the Channel.

It will have been noticed that Silver City drivers always drove the cars on and off the aircraft. This was essential because the width of the aircraft hold left very little clearance – particularly if the car was something like a Rolls-Royce or a Bentley. In fact, with some of the larger cars the doors could not be opened in the hold and the drivers had to exit through a sunroof or window, tactfully out of sight of the cars' owners. It was an advantage to be a gymnast if you were a Silver City driver! There was only one person who was allowed to drive his own car onto the aircraft himself – the Queen's chauffeur, who was considered to be sufficiently well trained.

To achieve the frequency of these flights the turn-around time for a Superfreighter from arrival to departure was critical. It was incredible that the time was actually reduced to eleven minutes.

After landing and just before turning onto the apron, the co-pilot would come down the crew ladder and unlatch all but one of the nose door latches. As soon as the aircraft came to a halt and the chocks were in place, the engines were stopped; the nose doors were opened, up went the ramps and in went the drivers who quickly drove the cars off down the ramps and into the 'Inbound' tunnel in the terminal. Meanwhile, the crews were disembarked and getting briefed for their next trip or going off duty, while the air hostess handed her passengers over to the ground hostess who whisked them away to the terminal. Within a few minutes, the boarding process was being repeated all over again.

Refuelling usually took place on every other round trip, but to make sure that the refuellers knew they were needed, a blue flag was put into a small bracket outside the cockpit window as the aircraft turned onto the apron. When the refuelling was finished, the flag was put *inside* the window to indicate that the process was complete.

As a footnote to those nose doors, it goes without saying that it was vitally important that they did not come open in flight. One operator had an incident where the doors opened at the start of the take-off run, which was quickly aborted – resulting in damage to the doors and propellers. As a result, a micro-switch was fitted to the doors which illuminated a warning light in the cockpit if the doors were not closed securely.

During 1957, the Air Ferry clocked up 1 million crossings of the Channel since its inception in 1948. In October the unbelievable happened. Taffy, as we have seen, was tireless in driving the company forward, but his health was failing and he was forced to retire on doctor's advice. The Welsh Dragon was gone. Bill Franklin and C.M. Fox became the joint managing directors. Air Kruise amalgamated with Silver City on 1 October 1957; their founder and managing director, Wing Commander Hugh Kennard, becoming deputy managing director of Silver City. The winter saw all the Air Kruise aircraft repainted into the silver, Royal blue and white of Silver City.

Also in October, Guernsey was closed to heavy aircraft like the Superfreighter while a new hard runway was constructed. The smaller de Havilland Herons continued a passenger-only service from Southampton; the new runway was not finished until 1959! Tragedy struck the British Aviation Services group on 15 November 1957 when one of Aquila's flying boats crashed into a hill on the Isle of Wight shortly after take-off from Southampton with the loss of forty-three lives. The 1957 traffic figures showed an increase in numbers but the revenue for the year had dropped.

Opposite: Passengers enjoy the Ferryfield sunshine while waiting for their flight.

Left: The Silver City brochure for 1957.

Opposite top: The Silver City air services network shown inside the company's 1957 brochure.

Opposite bottom: Passengers arrive in their car at the car park to the rear of the terminal building.

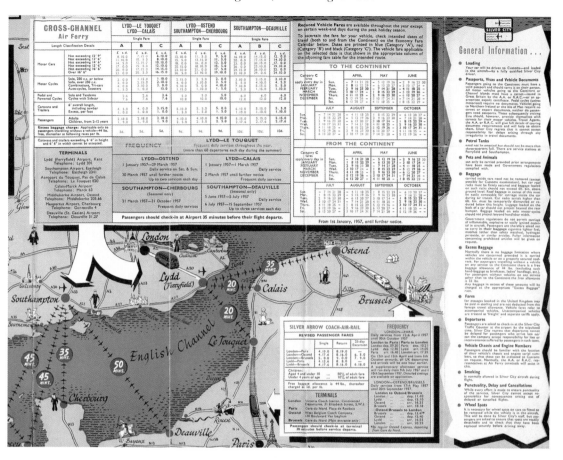

Passengers in the lounge waiting to be called for their flight.

The passengers' car in the 'Outbound' tunnel; AA or RAC staff check the vehicle's identity with the documentation. The Customs Officers check the baggage.

The cars are loaded on to the waiting aircraft by Silver City drivers.

Little room to spare in the hold!

The crew is on board, nose doors closed; now the passengers board. The tractor is attached ready to 'pull-back' the aircraft.

The Queen's car is driven on to the aircraft by the only non-Silver City driver allowed to do so – her chauffeur. The Queen's Rolls-Royce was on its way to Paris for her visit to France in 1957.

Above: The cockpit of a Bristol 170
Mk 32.

Right: The passenger cabin of a Bristol
170 Mk 32.

Bristol 170 Mk 21 G-AGVB in CAT livery; note the early blunt spinners.

Bristol 170 Mk 21 F-BHVB in CAT livery (1957).

Bristol 170 Mk 32 G-ANWK taxies to the runway.

Runway 25 at Le Touquet.

On the apron at Le Touquet.

At Le Touquet a French Customs Officer examines a passenger's 'Carnet'.

G-ANWG heads
a row of Mk 32s at
Ferryfield.

Air Kruise Dakota
before the repaint,
1957.

Another Air Kruise
Dakota, now in Silver
City livery, 1957.

Aquila's Short Solent flying boat G-AKNU that crashed on the Isle of Wight 15 November 1957.

Passengers board a Bristol 170 Mk 32 at Ferryfield.

Bristol 170 Mk 21 G-AGVC in Manx Airlines livery, 1957.

Bristol 170 Mk 21 G-AIFV with the Lancashire Aircraft Corporation (LAC) logo on the fin, 1957.

Manx Airlines and Lancashire Aircraft Corporation (LAC) individual timetables for 1957.

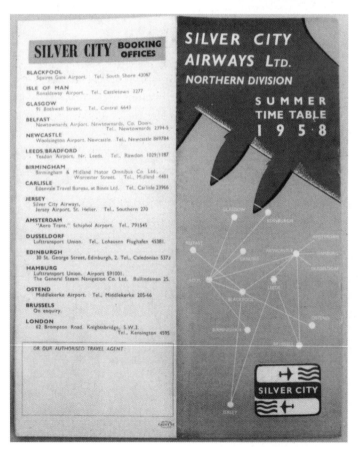

Silver City Northern Division timetable, 1958.

CHAPTER 10

A YEAR TO CELEBRATE

I n spite of the fall in revenue for 1957, Silver City persevered with the policy of 'low
fares – more customers' and dramatically reduced the fares for 1958 by up to 50 per
cent in some categories. This had the immediate effect of doubling the bookings.
Cherbourg was up 60 per cent and Ostend doubled – and this at the beginning of the
year. To use a previous example, the Morris Minor category fare from Ferryfield to Le
Touquet was now only £5 10s 0d (just under £100 today).

During the winter of 1957/58 the Superfreighters were given names of UK cities,
painted in blue on a white panel beneath the cockpit windows; G-AMWA, for example,
was named *City of London*. This brought them into line with the Mk 21s and Dakotas.
Air Kruise aircraft were repainted into the silver, Royal blue and white of Silver City.
In February, Silver City moved their Head Office to a new multi-storey building at
62 Brompton Road in London.

The same month, sadly, also witnessed the first fatality on a Silver City flight. A Mk
21, G-AICS, was en-route from Ronaldsway (Isle of Man) to Manchester, on charter to
a group of Motor Traders who were visiting the Exide battery factory in Manchester.
The aircraft strayed from its proper routing due to a misread Radio Beacon Identification
Coding and in low cloud crashed into the peak of Winter Hill near Chorley. Of the forty-
two on board, thirty-five were killed. Steve Morrin's book *The Devil Casts His Net* tells the
full story. In March, Silver City signed a lucrative contract with the Renault car company
to fly their new Dauphine model to the UK. Simca cars joined the imports a year later.

The Silver Arrow service from London to Paris was flourishing and more capacity
was needed to meet these demands. Initially, the problem was solved by the East Kent
Road Car Co. running several coaches in convoy to Ferryfield. Once at Ferryfield, the
passengers boarded a Superfreighter that had been modified with sixty of those 'bus-type'
seats described earlier and the journey continued. Two Superfreighters – G-AMWC
and G-AMWD – were modified; they became known as 'Super Wayfarers'. (The one
concession to luxury was a chrome-plated crew ladder!)

On 1 July 1958, Her Majesty Queen Elizabeth the Queen Mother arrived at Ferryfield,
having visited the Horticultural College at Wye in Kent. She was greeted by Wing

Commander Hugh Kennard on behalf of Silver City. After signing the Distinguished Visitors' Book she boarded the waiting Queen's Flight de Havilland Heron and flew on to Hullavington. Later, on 9 July, six aircraft of the Hermes fleet flew 241 members of the Huddersfield Choral Society, with their conductor Sir Malcolm Sargent, from Manchester to Brussels. They were performing at the Brussels International Fair and returned over 13 and 14 July.

14 July was also a date for celebration as it marked the 10th anniversary of the start of the Air Ferry. A multitude of dignitaries and Press reporters thronged the apron at Ferryfield. The VIPs were Dr J. Pouget (the Mayor of Le Touquet) and Alderman G.T. Paine (the Mayor of Lydd); Eoin Mekie, the Silver City chairman, was the chief company representative. The focus of the gathering was Superfreighter G-ANWK. The Mayor of Lydd unveiled the aircraft's name *The Fourteenth of July* newly painted just below the cockpit window on the starboard side. The party then flew on this aircraft to Le Touquet where the ceremony was repeated by the Mayor of Le Touquet, this time on the port side revealing *Le Quatorze Juillet*.

Silver City had been running a small operation in Libya for some time with a de Havilland Dragon Rapide based in Tripoli. This aircraft carried out work for some of the oil companies which were prospecting for oil in the Sahara Desert. In 1958, this operation started to grow rapidly but this will be covered in a later chapter.

The company's Northern Division was also very active. One of their new contracts was with the Nuclear Power Group to operate a passenger service between Manchester and Wick. The aircraft used were Dakotas or Herons and the service operated several times a week. Another of their passenger services was Blackpool to Ostend. At the end of September the Britavia group lost one of its number when Aquila Airways closed down. Flying boats had finally been superseded by jet airliners.

Silver City carried a huge variety of loads over the years; here are just a few examples:

Import and export cars;
Carpets;
Helicopters;
Two 60ft racing yacht hulls;
Yacht masts;
Printing presses;
Tractors;
Pigeons;
A midget submarine;
Race horses;
Every variety of four-legged beasts; and
a HUGE pink elephant (of the stuffed variety, belonging to a circus).

Believe it or not, some of these cargoes carried a few hazards for crew and aircraft alike. Sheep would try to graze the pilots' ankles as they climbed the crew ladder; pigs found the insulation around the navigation equipment cables running down the hold irresistible. When the hold was full of sheep, they inconsiderately got hot and steamy and the lanolin fumes from their wool seeped up into the cockpit and steamed up the windows, including the windscreen.

The name Silver City crept into the world of motor racing over the next three years when the company sponsored a Formula 1 race to be run at Brands Hatch in Kent; a handsome 'Silver City Trophy' awaited the winner. The event attracted all the top drivers and the 1961 race was won by none other than Stirling Moss driving a UDT-Laystall Lotus at an average speed of 91.78mph. Jim Clark was second, Tony Brooks third and Roy Salvadori fourth.

The number of cars carried during 1958 was 50,006 (60 per cent higher than the previous year). The revenue figures improved but not in proportion to the traffic.

Three Superfreighters at Le Touquet displaying their city names.

Above: The new Silver City House, Brompton Road Head Office.

Opposite top: Ford Anglia export cars.

Opposite bottom: The Super Wayfarer G-AMWD in passenger configuration.

Her Majesty Queen Elizabeth the Queen Mother signs the Distinguished Visitors' Book on 1 July 1958 at Ferryfield. Her Majesty was about to board a Queen's Flight de Havilland Heron after a visit to Wye Horticultural College.

Sheep in a Superfreighter hold.

Simca import cars.

Passengers queue to board the 'all-passenger' Super Wayfarer G-AMWD.

A Bristol 170 Mk 32 being refuelled at Ferryfield.

Stirling Moss holding the Silver City Trophy in 1961.

CHAPTER 11

WATER, WATER EVERYWHERE

1959 began in similar style to the previous year with yet another cut in fares; this time up to 25 per cent. The cross-Channel fare for a family Morris Minor was now only £5 0s 0d (equivalent to £85 today).

During the second week of March, the soggy runway conditions at Eastleigh proved too much and Silver City moved its Southampton services to Bournemouth (Hurn) with its concrete runway and better facilities. They returned to Eastleigh in June only to move back again to Hurn in November for the same reasons as before. Three Superfreighters were positioned at Hurn to meet the Air Ferry traffic requirements to Cherbourg and Deauville.

On 26 March, the company's Passenger Division at Ferryfield started operating 'No Passport Day Trips' between Ferryfield and Le Touquet for just 65 shillings (£3 5s 0d) using Dakota aircraft. This service operated until 3 September. 'Passenger Division' was a locally used term at Ferryfield to describe those staff involved in the passenger-only flights as distinct from Air Ferry activities. Meanwhile, Northern Division had been busy, too. In May, they opened a new passenger service operating a pool system with Aer Lingus and using Dakotas between Blackpool and Dublin. The Blackpool to the Isle of Man service was also doing well, operating over ten flights a day at peak times.

May 1959 saw yet another milestone for the Air Ferry service when Silver City flew their 250,000th car. Appropriately enough, it was flown by Captain Jerry Rosser who had been on the inaugural flight from Lympne eleven years before. July produced some spectacular events at Ferryfield to mark the 50th anniversary of the first crossing of the Channel by Louis Blériot in 1909. As part of the celebrations, the *Daily Mail* offered a prize of £5,000 to the person who could travel fastest between London's Marble Arch and the Arc de Triomphe in Paris (or vice-versa). There were many entrants; Silver City entered in partnership with Formula 1 motor-racing legend Stirling Moss.

Moss drove a Renault Dauphine Gordini at 'white-knuckle speed' – the passenger's own words – from London to Ferryfield. Waiting for him – doors open, ramp in place and engines running – was a Silver City Superfreighter. Quick as a flash, Moss was in and the aircraft was on its way – with another hairy ride to come for the unfortunate passenger, from the airport at Le Touquet to the centre of Paris. It should be noted that it was strictly taboo to run an aircraft's engines with a nose door open but an exception was made in this case.

The race was won (in the Paris–London direction) by a team led by Squadron Leader C.G. Maughan, the CO of No.65 Squadron at Duxford, using an RAF Police motorcycle, a Bristol Sycamore helicopter and a Hawker Hunter T7 in an overall time of forty minutes and forty-four seconds. Another event linked to the anniversary was the arrival on 15 July of a replica Blériot monoplane from Cap Blanc Nez near Calais. It was flown by a Frenchman, Monsieur Jean Salis. The landing was watched with interest as the machine had no brakes; however, all was well and M. Salis was greeted by a crowd of well-wishers. Perhaps he was not too keen to repeat the experience because the Silver City engineers soon took the aircraft to pieces and loaded it onto a Superfreighter, whereupon pilot and machine were flown back to Calais courtesy of Captain Terry Mattock.

Movements of commercial aircraft at Blackbushe airport were falling off and there was talk of it closing that winter. Silver City based their Handley Page Hermes aircraft there, as they were too big for Ferryfield. So now the question arose as to what to do with them. The company successfully negotiated a deal with the Ministry of Defence who owned RAF Manston near Ramsgate in Kent. RAF Manston was a Master Diversion airport with a massively long and wide runway. During the summer and autumn the four remaining Hermes were moved to Manston and transferred from Britavia's books to Silver City's. At the same time, the livery of three of the aircraft was also changed to that of Silver City. On 15 June, the Hermes replaced the Bristol 170s on the Silver Arrow service; the benefits being their extra capacity and comfort. However, they were more expensive to operate on such a short route. The coach journey from London to Margate was replaced by a train service. The Silver City record book had another entry when, on 18 September, it flew its one millionth passenger.

We are now moving into the autumn and winter of 1959 and it was decided that the Bristol 170 fleet needed a fresh paint scheme to replace the existing bare metal and medium blue livery. This would be applied during the winter heavy maintenance period. The Superfreighters were to have a white fuselage top, including the fin, then a wide band of a brighter Royal blue extending down the fuselage side to within 4ft of the bottom – the last 4ft being polished aluminium. The wings and tailplane were unpolished natural metal. The Mk 21s were to have a similar scheme but appeared with two thinner Royal blue lines separated by a light grey band about 4ft wide. The lower part of the fuselage was also light grey.

After this 'mass paint job' it was uncanny to see that some Silver City employees' houses now gleamed with fresh white, Royal blue or Brunswick green paint! Brunswick green, oddly enough, was the colour of some parts of the Dakota! The new colour schemes suited the aircraft very well and they all looked very smart when they came back into service.

Having made the point that the aircraft looked good on the outside, on wet days the story was very different on the inside. Due to the method of construction, the fact that they were getting older and that they had been taken apart a few times, it was hardly surprising that they leaked a bit. The aft passenger cabin fared reasonably well but in the cockpit it was another matter; it has been said that a sieve held more water than the cockpit of a Superfreighter. The pilots therefore had to be prepared to meet this challenge. The first line of defence was to take on board the thickest newspaper you could find – that's why so many of the pilots took *The Times* and the *Financial Times*. (The latter was said to have a magnificent absorption rate!)

The second line was to wear some waterproof clothing; indeed, on a really bad winter's day, the crew looked as if they should be heading for the Dungeness Lifeboat rather than an aeroplane as they walked across to their waiting aircraft. The Mk 21s, of course, carried passengers in the hold and heavy rain could be bad news for them. Where the wings joined the fuselage was a real trouble spot and in spite of the engineers' best efforts to seal it, water often found its way in. If any water got in it gathered out of sight in the roof trim. Here any red hydraulic oil that had leaked from the auto-pilot servomotors would also gather.

On one flight to Ostend, the ceiling of one Mk 21 could finally cope with no more and emptied its mixture of water and hydraulic oil over Rows 6 and 7 – much to the surprise and horror of the doused passengers. The hostess quickly brought the situation under control, cleaning everybody and everything in no time. She was a resourceful girl and using the *Financial Times* and other quality papers made a most competent papier mâché repair to the ceiling. The passengers, of course, were given profuse apologies and well compensated for any damage and inconvenience.

The year end saw another marked increase in traffic numbers.

A Silver City 'No Passport' flight Dakota.

Stirling Moss barely on four wheels as the joint Silver City/Moss entry for the *Daily Mail* London to Paris Air Race arrives on the Ferryfield apron.

The *Daily Mail* London to Paris Air Race. Stirling Moss boards at speed in the Renault Dauphine Gordini.

Another contestant in the *Daily Mail* London to Paris Air Race, 1959.

Ferryfield, 15 July 1959. M. Jean Salis flew his replica Blériot monoplane into the airport to celebrate the 50th anniversary of the first Channel crossing by air in 1909.

The Blériot replica was dismantled and flown back to Calais in a Superfreighter.

Silver City's Handley Page Hermes G-ALDM at Manston in 1959.

Hermes G-ALDP in the hangar at Manston.

Superfreighter G-AMWB resplendent in its new livery at Ferryfield in 1959.

Three Bristol 170 Mk 21s at Ferryfield in their final liveries: G-AIME, G-AIFM and G-AHJI.

A trial livery was applied to Superfreighters G-AMWF and G-ANWJ during 1959.

Another 'oddity' was the 'half and half' logo on G-ANWI. Coincidentally, the Superfreighter in the background at Le Touquet is G-AMWF in its 'trial' livery.

The Fokker F27 Friendship demonstrator PH–NVF arrives at Ferryfield in 1959.

Engineering manager Bill Kerr talks to a Straits Air Freight Express (SAFE) crew from New Zealand. Silver City engineering staff are going to carry out some maintenance on their aircraft.

King Hussein of Jordan with Hugh Kennard at Ferryfield, 29 November 1959.

Lord Douglas of Kirtleside (Chairman of BEA) arrives at Ferryfield (1959).

CHAPTER 12

OIL AND SAND

In an earlier chapter we saw the beginning of Silver City's involvement in Libya with a de Havilland Dragon Rapide. Let's turn the clock back to Libya in 1957; the work had built up to a level that required the use of a Dakota or Bristol 170 aircraft. This aircraft was provided on an 'as required' basis from the UK but the amount of work got to a point where this was no longer viable and it was decided that an 'Out Station Group' should be established in Tripoli and later a second, smaller Group in Benghazi.

The work was certainly varied. At first it was mainly carrying geologists and seismic survey parties all over the country; sometimes as far as the Chad border. Navigating over long distances without any form of radio aids was an experience not to be missed. Later, when oil was found, there were oil and water drilling sites to be supplied with food and whatever else they required – the loads ranged from Land Rover engines to camp personnel. The French camps were interesting as their staff favoured livestock in their food supplies. Cages of pigeons, fowl, rabbits and, on one occasion, a small pig were carried. Inevitably the pig broke free!

It was not uncommon for an aircraft to be required at short notice to hunt for oil workers lost in the desert. Some VIP flights were undertaken too for the family of King Idris who reigned at the time.

Alan Offer, a Silver City engineer, tells of his experiences with the Group:

The major maintenance was still carried out at Ferryfield but all the other maintenance including scheduled engine changes was done by the Silver City engineers in the Group at Castel Benito airfield – ten miles inland from Tripoli. The Group numbered up to eighteen engineers, twelve pilots and a small admin staff headed by Freddie Foster. The Chief Pilot was Captain 'Hoppy' Hopkins and the Chief Engineers over the period from 1957 to 1961 were Ron Townsend, 'Jock' Colquhoun and Edwin Egget.

The Group operated with an average of seven aircraft – a mixture of de Havilland Doves, Douglas Dakotas and Bristol 170 Mk 21s. Quite often, repairs had to be made away from the Tripoli base with the minimum of equipment. Engine changes were among the most testing but on one occasion an incredible feat of engineering was undertaken at 'Bled Total', a French oil-drilling camp. It involved our Dakota, G-AOBN.

Before going out to Libya the aircraft had gone to Marshall of Cambridge to have special wing modifications done. A few weeks later, the Air Registration Board (predecessors of the present Civil Aviation Authority), advised Silver City that a number of rivets had been left out of the modification and that wherever the aircraft was it had to be grounded immediately. This is not good news when your aircraft is in the middle of the desert and the wings have to be taken off and put back on again! This would not be the easiest of jobs in the hangar – but in the desert!!! Two of Marshall's engineers were quickly despatched to 'Bled Total' and somehow, between them, the Silver City engineers and a mobile crane, they did the job.

As with a lot of small outstations, a very good *esprit de corps* developed and, to show their individual identity, a blue camel logo had been painted on the nose of the aircraft. When visiting Silver City management saw it they were not impressed and requested its removal.

In 1959 Silver City carried out trials with a French Hurel-Dubois HD.34, an unusual-looking aeroplane with a long, narrow 'plank'-like wing on top of the fuselage which gave it a remarkably short take-off and landing capability. It was also ideal for the long-duration, slow-speed flight needed when undertaking survey work. However, Silver City did not order any and indeed only eight were ever built.

A Dakota crew on a flight from Kufra Oasis spotted the wreck of an American Liberator bomber the *Lady Be Good*. It had force-landed in the desert after a bombing raid on Naples in April 1943. The book *Lady's Men* by Mario Martinez and a website of the same name details this fascinating story.

The Out Station Group was disbanded in 1961 when, due to the civil war in the Congo, the Belgian airline Sabena found their aircraft out of work and were able to outbid Silver City for the Libyan contract.

A South African DC3 ZS-DDC leased by Silver City for the Libyan operations.

A DC2 ZS-DFX also leased from South Africa for Libyan operations.

A DC3 engine change in the desert.

DC3 G-AMYX in front of the pre-war Italian hangar at Kufra. Note the controversial 'camel' logo on the nose of the aircraft.

Bristol 170 Mk 21 G-AHJI at work for Shell in the desert.

DC3 G-AOBN with its wings removed in the desert.

The Hurel-Dubois HD.34 F-BICU at Tripoli June 1959. The aircraft was the seventh production aircraft and was on a short lease to Silver City for evaluation.

Silver City de Havilland Dove G-AOYC at Idris. The engineer is Vic Farish.

CHAPTER 13

AN UNLUCKY NUMBER?

B y 1960, Silver City had become a household name. For a lot of families, taking their car to the Continent on the Air Ferry was the first time they had flown. The airline not only had family appeal but many members of Royal Families, stars of stage and screen, politicians and other celebrities all used the Air Ferry as the best way to cross the Channel.

Manston was very busy with the Hermes fleet operating charter and inclusive tour flights to a wide variety of destinations in Europe and sometimes beyond. These aircraft were also still on the 'Silver Arrow' service to Paris for which the fare was now £9 9s 0d, just £1 more than the boat fare and equivalent to about £160 today. Later in the year, the Hermes were heavily involved in a Ministry of Defence contract to carry servicemen to and from Germany. The Hermes activity at Manston was joined by a Superfreighter; it was positioned there to operate the Ostend route that had been transferred from Ferryfield. This shortened the flight time by ten minutes and proved very popular, doubling the traffic to Ostend by the end of the year.

Meanwhile, at Ferryfield, Silver City claimed another bizarre first when it opened a zoo, the only airport in the world to have such a thing. It was at the far west end of the terminal building; clearly the object of it was to entertain waiting children. It was run by the Chipperfields, the well-known circus family. However, it was strange to see chimpanzees, llamas, a bear and a kangaroo gazing across the tarmac.

In June, the company extended its 'No Passport' trips by offering a two-day break in Paris. The Hurn base was buzzing too; Bryan Keeping, one of the flight attendants who operated from there, wrote:

> In 1960 I earned £8 5s 0d a week. There was a flight every thirty minutes between eight in the morning and six in the evening. The fare for a medium size car was £10 0s 0d and £4 13s 0d per passenger. Our cruising speed was 165 miles per hour.
>
> If there were no drivers available on the ground, I had to drive the cars on and off. On one occasion, an aircraft engine starter would not work and, believe it or not, we started it by putting a rope round the propeller blade and pulling; the passengers thought it hilarious.

Air Traffic Control was not overly busy and sometimes the only take-off clearance was: 'You are free to go to London.'

The Cherbourg route carried some 10,000 cars in 1960. Silver City aircraft crossing the Channel also performed another useful service by keeping an eye on shipping. Quite often they were able to report a tanker flushing its tanks or report a ship in distress to the maritime authorities.

November saw one of the Dakotas – G-AOBN – begin a contract to check and calibrate Radio Aids in the UK and in many other parts of the world. The aircraft went to Biggin Hill to be fitted with the special equipment needed to do the job; 'Nobby' Clarke was the calibration engineer who flew with the aircraft. Because this aircraft was so busy it had minimal time for maintenance and overruns were to be avoided if at all possible. As a result, engineering overtime flowed like nectar when the aircraft with its distinctive 'Day-Glo' orange nose and fin-tip appeared at Ferryfield.

At Christmas time, Silver City were very generous to their staff by giving each person a hamper full of Christmas fare – these hampers appeared in the bonded store a week or so before Christmas. From the first week in December, the main topic of conversation at Ferryfield was the arrival or – heaven forbid – non-arrival of the hampers. Rumours spread like wildfire from most departments that the hampers had been seen in the most unlikely places.

During the year around 90,000 vehicles and 220,000 passengers had been carried and 40,000 Channel crossings had been made. Freight too was up to a staggering 135,000 tons, an increase of some 35 per cent on the previous year. The Manston to Ostend Air Ferry service had seen a huge jump in traffic, doubling the Ferryfield to Ostend numbers of the previous year. Another Air Ferry star performer was the Hurn–Cherbourg route which had increased its traffic by a third to 10,000 vehicles. Fares were lowered again for the 1961 season with a reduction to £4 0s 0d (equivalent to £68 today) for a family-size car while motorcycles under 250cc cost a miniscule 2s 6d (12.5p or about £2 today). In February, a weekly service started between Guernsey and Cherbourg using a Hurn-based Superfreighter.

The Ferryfield summer traffic was very much as normal for the season with no outstanding events. Early in the summer, Silver City had concluded a deal with Compagnie Air Transport (CAT) – a subsidiary of a large road haulage company – for them to build a two-mile spur from the nearby main railway line into Le Touquet Airport. This would greatly enhance the Silver Arrow service. In exchange, Silver City would transfer three of its Superfreighters to CAT for them to operate on the Ferryfield–Le Touquet and Hurn–Cherbourg routes. The aircraft livery would be identical to Silver City's except that the name was changed and the Union Flag was replaced by a Tricolour on the fin. The aircraft were to be flown by French CAT crews whose Gauloises cigarette aroma betrayed their presence in the cockpit.

Silver City were still very aware of the need to extend the range of the Air Ferry deeper into Europe. The problem, as we saw before, was the lack of a suitable new larger aircraft. The usual manufacturers had failed to come up with an affordable solution. Freddie

Laker and his Channel Air Bridge were facing the same dilemma and it was his company – Aviation Traders (Engineering) Ltd (ATL) – that provided an answer. ATL had a design and manufacturing capability at Southend and they worked out a new design based on the existing Douglas DC4 aircraft.

The major part of the conversion consisted of cutting off the nose and replacing it with a single hinged nose door. The cockpit was repositioned on top of the enlarged nose – Boeing 747-style – and a larger fin was fitted for improved directional stability. These changes gave the aircraft a hold capable of carrying five cars and twenty passengers in its Air Ferry configuration. The aircraft was known as the ATL-98 or 'Carvair' and it flew for the first time on 22 June 1961. Second-hand DC4s were plentiful and cheap to buy, so a Carvair would cost just £150,000. It was powered by four Pratt & Whitney R-2000 Twin Wasp engines giving 1,450hp at take-off. The aircraft had a speed of 200mph and a range of 250 nautical miles.

Towards the end of the year, Silver City applied to fly scheduled passenger flights between a number of the airports served by its Northern Division. The application included provision for the routes to be operated by Vickers Viscount aircraft as well as the Dakotas! With this in mind, the company leased three ex-Air France Viscount 708 turboprop aircraft from Maitland Drewery Aviation. These forty-nine-seat aircraft went to Fields Aircraft Services at Wymeswold to be refurbished and repainted in Silver City livery.

1 November 1961 was a tragic day for the airline when Superfreighter G-ANWL crashed. It was carrying out a 'missed approach' procedure while landing at Guernsey, inbound from Cherbourg. The pilot – Captain George Hogarth (who was chief pilot at Hurn) – and his co-pilot Derek Cornford-Evans were both killed; seven passengers were injured. The ensuing investigation concluded that a malfunction in the Automatic Pitch Coarsening system associated with the starboard propeller was the cause of the crash. This deepened the gloom that surrounded the company amidst persistent rumours that a merger with Freddie Laker's Channel Air Bridge was in the wind.

The 1961 traffic figures looked good with just over 96,000 vehicles carried – including 16,900 exports as well as 14,000 from Hurn – and 238,000 passengers; all from 43,000 crossings of the Channel. However, the little-known truth was that Silver City had made a loss of £250,000 in 1960 and 1961 was little better with a loss of £200,000. That was a lot to lose in those days.

The air of gloom continued into 1962. In January, unknown to the staff, British Aviation Services (Silver City's parent company) decided to sell its shares to P&O. This enabled P&O to set up a new company – Air Holdings Ltd. They took over British Aviation Services, Channel Air Bridge and the newly formed British United Airways together with its associated companies. The news was released to the Silver City staff in February; Silver City's thirteen-year adventure was over.

In those thirteen years, Silver City had provided a unique service that had developed into a huge operation, the like of which will probably never be seen again. Friendly, personal and efficient service plus an excellent safety record has ensured that their passengers still look back on them with fondness and respect.

Film star Diana Dors.

Film star David Niven with his wife.

Lord Brabazon of Tara (holder of the first pilot's certificate in Great Britain) with his Jaguar.

Film star Gregory Peck with Silver City's Captain Terry Mattock.

A Bristol 170 Mk 32 at Manston.

DC3 G-AOBN – the Radio Calibration Unit aircraft.

Bristol 170 Mk 32 F-BLHH in Compagnie Air Transport (CAT) livery.

A British United ATL-98 Carvair G-ASDC; the first Carvair to operate from Ferryfield in 1962.

A very rare picture of a freshly painted Silver City Viscount 708. The aircraft did not enter service with Silver City but was absorbed into the British United Airways fleet following the merger in 1962.

Silver City souvenirs were sold in the airport shop. (Examples of most of these are in the Silver City Association collection.)

Photograph of British Aviation Services (Engineering) Ltd staff taken 23 March 1962 prior to closure of the Manston, Kent, base. Hermes aircraft G-ALDG – *City of Chester* in the background. Names of staff – from left to right:

R. Horsley (Engine Fitter), D. Baigent (Senior Technical Records Clerk), L. Scott (Airframe Inspector), S. Syposz (Airframe Fitter), J. Jones (Airframe Fitter), C. Lock (Upholsterer), N. Bennett (Tarmac Engineering Supervisor), A. Ayres (Airframe Fitter), B. Philpott (Airframe Charge-hand), H. Burgess (Instrument Charge-hand), K. Lee (Senior (Hangar) Charge-hand), A. Hunt (Tractor Driver), W. Smith (M.T. Charge-hand), F. Strainge (Electrical Charge-hand/Inspector), J. Burton (Engine Fitter), K. Singh (Engine Fitter), J. Duffy (Aircraft Refueller), F. Ansell (Maintenance Foreman), J. Mason (Radio Mechanic), R. Illsley (Engineering Manager), T. Stokes (Cabin Cleaner), J. Harrop (Engine Inspector), P. Goddard (Secretary to Engineering Manager), K. Edgar (Engine Charge-hand), R. Smith (Aircraft Refueller), E. Sadler (Power Plant Bay Leading-hand), P. Rigby (Planning Engineer), W. Darch (Aircraft Cleaner), S. Earll (Aircraft Cleaner), Mrs K. Drew (Stock Records Department), G. Hunter (Carpenter), J. Clarke (Cabin Cleaner), G. Littlewood (Supplies Officer), A. Noller (Radio Mechanic), S. Young (Stores Assistant), J. Hunt (Electrician), R. Dewhurst (Stores Driver), R. Hampton (Stores Assistant), S. Lovett (Stores Assistant), A. O'Reilly (Engine Leading-hand), B. Smith (Stores Assistant), J. Liddle (Labour Group Leader), L. Mees (Engine Fitter), J. Verrion (Aircraft Refu eller), R. Bedford (Electrician), S. Goodbourn (Aircraft Cleaner), R. Wickens (Engine Fitter), J. Goodfellow (Engine Fitter Power Plants), W. Twyman (Aircraft Cleaner), L. Knight (Storekeeper-in-Charge), S. Walker (Aircraft Refueller), H. Turvey (Engine Fitter).

Left: A group of engineers at Manston.

Below: A line-up of three Bristol 170 Mk 32s at Ferryfield in the final Silver City livery (1960).

EPILOGUE

Although Silver City had gone, the Air Ferry continued at Ferryfield with other operators for another nine years. The last Bristol 170 flight from there was in October 1970 and the last Carvair flight a year later – but that's another story. So what caused Silver City's demise? As in so many cases there was no single reason. The main factor was that the short routes such as Ferryfield to Le Touquet were heavy on aircraft wear and hence costs – the answer was to operate on longer routes but, as seen, there was no suitable aircraft available at the time it was needed. The boat ferries were also now larger and more attractive, though the convenience factor of the Air Ferry largely counteracted this. Finally, perhaps one has to question the wisdom of the company policy of consistent price cutting; who knows?

What happened to some of the people featured in this book? Bert Hayes, the Shacklip inventor, went on to become a BAC 1-11 captain with British Caledonian Airways; Dave Flett became a senior pilot on British United's VC10 fleet, while Jerry Rosser became a Silver City training captain and retired when Silver City closed. Alan Offer continued his engineering career with Sudan Airways. Wing Commander Hugh Kennard and his wife Audrey went on to form Air Ferry and later Invicta Airways at Manston. Bill Kerr became the Base Engineering Manager with BUA/BCAL at Gatwick.

The spirit of Silver City that was so evident during those halcyon years survives today in the Silver City Association. The Association has a membership of over 200 ex-Silver City employees and others involved with the Air Ferry, together with a growing band of Silver City enthusiasts. There is an Annual Reunion at Lydd (Ferryfield) which is regularly attended by about 100 'citizens'; those who cannot be there keep in touch through the Association's newsletter. The Association also holds what is probably the most comprehensive collection of original documents, photographs and Silver City memorabilia in the world.

The last word of course has to be Taffy's and our tale ends with this story. Sadly Taffy Powell died in 1999 at the age of ninety-one. Because of his rank of Air Commodore, he was entitled to have his funeral at St Clement Danes – the Central Church of the Royal Air Force in London. The funeral service was scheduled to begin at twelve noon but 12:15 came and went with no sign of Taffy. A few minutes later, an usher went up to Taffy's son Wyndham and whispered in his ear. Wyndham turned round and said, 'You'll never believe this but Taffy's got stuck on Westminster Bridge in a bomb scare'. He would be furious at being late for his own funeral – someone would be sacked!

APPENDIX 1

FLEET LIST – AIR KRUISE (KENT) LTD

AUSTER J/1 AUTOCRAT
G-AIZZ – c/n 2234

Purchased by Wing Commander Kennard
   on 21/09/49
Transferred to Skyfotos Ltd on 26/04/61

BRISTOL 170 FREIGHTER MK 21
G-AIFM – c/n 12773

Purchased by Air Kruise on 07/01/56
Transferred to Silver City Airways on
   08/10/57

G-AIME – C/N 12795

Purchased by Silver City Airways on
   21/11/50
Transferred to Air Kruise on 09/02/56
Returned to Silver City Airways on
   01/10/57

BRISTOL 170 FREIGHTER MK 21E
G-AHJI – c/n 12741

Purchased by Silver City Airways on
   10/12/55
Leased to Air Kruise on 21/12/55
Returned to Silver City Airways on
   01/10/57

DE HAVILLAND DH89A DRAGON RAPIDE
G-AESR – c/n 6363

Purchased by Air Kruise on 18/03/53
Leased to Oilfields Supply & Trading Co.
   (Benghazi, Libya) in 1956
Crashed and written-off at Gerdes el Abid
   on 22/09/56

G-AEWL – c/n 6367   *Nicole*

Purchased by Wing Commander Kennard
   on 13/04/50
Transferred to Air Kruise on 13/04/55
Sold to Aviation Supplies Co. Ltd on
   24/11/55

G-ALWK – c/n 6856

Purchased by Wing Commander Kennard
   on 21/08/51
Transferred to Air Kruise on 25/02/55
Returned to Wing Commander Kennard on
   08/08/55
Sold to Algeria on 15/04/57

DOUGLAS C-47A DAKOTA
G-ANLF – c/n 11979

Purchased by Air Kruise on 20/04/55
Transferred to Silver City Airways on
   28/10/57

DOUGLAS C-47B DAKOTA

G-AMYV – c/n 32943 *City of Oxford*

Purchased by Silver City Airways on
01/04/53

Transferred to Silver City Airways (Libya)
Ltd for remainder of 1953

Transferred to Air Kruise on 30/01/56

Returned to Silver City Airways on
28/10/57

G-AMYX – c/n 33042 *City of Rochester*

Purchased by Silver City Airways on
01/04/53

Transferred to Air Kruise on 30/01/56

Returned to Silver City Airways on
28/10/57

G-AMZB – c/n 26980

Purchased by Manx Airlines on 26/03/53

Transferred to Air Kruise on 06/11/56

Transferred to Silver City Airways on
28/10/57

DOUGLAS C-53D DAKOTA

G-AOBN – c/n 11711

Purchased by Air Kruise on 20/04/55

Transferred to Silver City Airways on
28/10/57

MILES M38 MESSENGER 2A

G-AHZS – c/n 6331

Registered by Wing Commander Kennard
on 19/07/46

Withdrawn from use and scrapped at
Ramsgate in August 1962

MILES M65 GEMINI 1A

G-AJWH – c/n 6293

Purchased by Wing Commander Kennard
on 31/01/51

Sold to Shackleton Aviation Ltd on
04/11/57

APPENDIX 2

FLEET LIST – BRITISH AVIATION SERVICES LTD AND BRITAVIA LTD

AIRSPEED AS65 CONSUL

G-AHRK – c/n 3096

Registered by British Aviation Services on
18/06/46

Transferred to British Aviation Services
(Malta) Ltd in January 1947

Sold to Malaya on 04/02/49

G-AIBF – c/n 3422

Registered by British Aviation Services on
30/07/46

Transferred to British Aviation Services
(Malta) Ltd in January 1947

Transferred to Silver City Airways on
02/05/49

G-AIKY – c/n 4324

Purchased by British Aviation Services on
06/12/46

Sold abroad on 09/04/47

G-AJGH – c/n 5124

Purchased by British Aviation Services on
29/03/47

Sold to Air Charter Ltd on 15/04/48

G-AJNG – c/n 5146

Purchased by British Aviation Services on
24/11/48

Sold to Airtech Ltd 02/07/49

AVRO 691 LANCASTRIAN 3

G-AHBT – c/n 1288   *City of New York*

Purchased by British Aviation Services on
17/08/46

Operated by Silver City Airways

Sold to Skyways Ltd on 06/06/47

G-AHBV – c/n 1290   *City of Canberra*

Purchased by British Aviation Services on
10/10/46

Operated by Silver City Airways

Transferred to Silver City Airways on
26/09/47

G-AHBW – c/n 1291   *City of London*

Purchased by British Aviation Services on
10/10/46

Operated by Silver City Airways

Sold to Australia on 21/01/48

BEECHCRAFT C-18S EXPEDITER

G-AKCZ – c/n 6116

Purchased by Britavia on 13/02/50

Sold to Northern Rhodesia on 14/08/50

BRISTOL 170 FREIGHTER MK 21

G-AIME – c/n 12795

Leased by British Aviation Services from The
Bristol Aeroplane Co. Ltd on 16/07/48

Returned in 1949

DE HAVILLAND DH104 DOVE 1
G-AIWF – c/n 04023
Purchased by British Aviation Services on
20/11/46
Transferred to Silver City Airways on
21/01/48

DOUGLAS C-47A DAKOTA
G-AIRG – c/n 25288
Purchased by British Aviation Services on
24/09/46
Transferred to Silver City Airways on
25/11/46

G-AIRH – c/n 12445
Purchased by Britavia on 24/09/46
Transferred to Silver City Airways on
19/10/46
Transferred to British Aviation Services (Air
Charter and Exploration) in October 1948
Sold to Africair Ltd on 23/07/49

G-AJZD – c/n 12333
Purchased by British Aviation Services on
18/06/47
Transferred to Silver City Airways on
18/02/48

DOUGLAS C-47B DAKOTA
G-AGNG – c/n 26998
Purchased by Britavia on 24/01/51
Transferred to Gulf Aviation Ltd on 10/02/51

G-AKAR – c/n 26889
Purchased by Britavia on 20/12/50
Sold to Air Carriers Supply Corporation on
01/01/51

HANDLEY PAGE HP81 HERMES 4
G-ALDI – c/n HP81/10
Purchased by Britavia on 19/06/54
Transferred to Silver City Airways in
September 1959

G-ALDJ – c/n HP81/11
Purchased by Britavia on 22/05/54
Crashed and written-off at Blackbushe on
06/11/56

G-ALDK – c/n HP81/12
Purchased by Britavia on 03/06/54
Damaged beyond repair and written-off
near Karachi on 05/08/56

G-ALDM – c/n HP81/14
Leased by Britavia from Air Safaris Ltd in
November 1956
Transferred to Silver City Airways on
15/06/59

G-ALDP – c/n HP81/17
Purchased by Britavia on 28/06/54
Transferred to Silver City Airways on
15/06/59

G-ALDU – c/n HP81/21
Purchased by Britavia on 27/05/54
Leased to Kuwait Airways on 20/05/56
Returned on 07/12/56
Transferred to Silver City Airways in July
1959

G-ALDX – c/n HP81/24
Purchased by Britavia on 31/05/54
Leased to Kuwait Airways on 29/05/56
Returned on 20/12/56
Transferred to Silver City Airways in August
1959

LOCKHEED L-14H ELECTRA
G-AGBG – c/n 1421
Purchased by British Aviation Services on
25/02/46
Sold to Southampton Air Services Ltd on
30/01/47

LOCKHEED L-18H LODESTAR
G-AJAW – c/n 1954
Registered by British Aviation Services on
18/01/47
Transferred to Silver City Airways on
20/01/48

APPENDIX 3

FLEET LIST – SILVER CITY AIRWAYS LTD

AIRSPEED AS65 CONSUL

G-AHRK – c/n 3096

Registered by British Aviation Services on
18/06/46

Transferred to British Aviation Services
(Malta) Ltd in January 1947

Sold to Malaya on 04/02/49

Purchased by Silver City Airways and
re-registered on 23/09/49

Sold to Spain on 05/03/52

G-AIBF – c/n 3422

Registered by British Aviation Services on
30/07/46

Transferred to British Aviation Services
(Malta) Ltd in January 1947

Transferred to Silver City Airways on
02/05/49

Withdrawn from use and scrapped at
Blackbushe on 19/02/54

G-AIUS – c/n 750

Purchased by Silver City Airways on
08/03/54

Sold on 13/06/58

AVRO 691 LANCASTRIAN 3

G-AHBT – c/n 1288   *City of New York*

Purchased by British Aviation Services on
17/08/46

Operated by Silver City Airways

Sold to Skyways Ltd on 06/06/47

G-AHBV – c/n 1290   *City of Canberra*

Purchased by British Aviation Services on
10/10/46

Operated by Silver City Airways

Transferred to Silver City Airways on
26/09/47

Sold to Aeronautical and Industrial Research
Corporation Ltd on 06/05/48

G-AHBW – c/n 1291   *City of London*

Purchased by British Aviation Services on
10/10/46

Operated by Silver City Airways

Sold to Australia on 21/01/48

BREGUET BR761S 'DEUX PONTS'

F-BASL – c/n 02

Leased by Silver City Airways from Breguet
in June 1953

Returned in September 1953

BRISTOL 170 FREIGHTER MK I

G-AGVC – c/n 12732   *City of Sheffield*

Leased by Silver City Airways from The
Bristol Aeroplane Co. Ltd on 06/07/48

Returned in February 1949 and converted
to Mk 21

Re-leased on 12/02/52

Purchased by Silver City Airways on
19/06/53

Leased to Manx Airlines Ltd in May 1956

Returned to Silver City Airways in 1958

Damaged beyond repair at Ronaldsway, Isle of Man on 30/06/62

BRISTOL 170 FREIGHTER MK IIA

G-AHJC – c/n 12735

Leased by Silver City Airways from The Bristol Aeroplane Co. Ltd on 18/09/48

Returned on 24/11/48

G-AHJG – c/n 12739

Leased by Silver City Airways from The Bristol Aeroplane Co. Ltd on 18/10/47

Returned in August 1948

G-AHJO – c/n 12747

Leased by Silver City Airways from Bowmaker Ltd on 14/09/48

Returned in early 1949

BRISTOL 170 FREIGHTER MK 21

G-AGVB – c/n 12731

Leased by Silver City Airways from Bowmaker Ltd on 28/07/49

Purchased by Silver City Airways on 03/04/54

Sold to Compagnie Air Transport on 06/02/57 as F-BHVB

G-AHJD – c/n 12736

Leased by Silver City Airways from Airwork Ltd in 1948

Leased by Silver City Airways from Eagle Aircraft Services Ltd in 1956

G-AICM – c/n 12756

Leased by Silver City Airways from The Bristol Aeroplane Co. Ltd in April 1951

Crashed and written-off at Tempelhof, Berlin, on 19/01/53

G-AIFM – c/n 12773   *City of Carlisle*

Purchased by Silver City Airways from Compagnie Air Transport in October 1951 as F-BEND

Sold in December 1951

Purchased by Air Kruise on 07/01/56

Transferred to Silver City Airways on 08/10/57

Transferred to British United Air Ferries Ltd on 01/01/63

Withdrawn from use at Lydd in November 1963 and broken up at Southend in October 1964

G-AIFV – c/n 12781   *City of Manchester*

Leased by Silver City Airways from The Bristol Aeroplane Co. Ltd

Purchased by Silver City Airways on 19/06/53

Withdrawn from use at Lydd in October 1961 and broken up in May 1962

G-AIME – c/n 12795   *City of Exeter*

Leased by British Aviation Services from The Bristol Aeroplane Co. Ltd on 16/07/48

Returned in 1949

Purchased by Silver City Airways on 21/11/50

Transferred to Air Kruise on 09/02/56

Returned to Silver City Airways on 01/10/57

Transferred to British United Air Ferries Ltd on 01/01/63

Withdrawn from use at Lydd in October 1963 and broken up at Southend in May 1964

G-AIMH – c/n 12798   *City of Birmingham*

Purchased by Silver City Airways from Compagnie Air Transport on 01/04/52 as F-BECT

Leased to Manx Airlines Ltd in May 1956

Returned to Silver City Airways in 1958

Withdrawn from use at Lydd in October 1962 and broken up in 1963

BRISTOL 170 FREIGHTER MK 21E

G-AHJI – c/n 12741   *City of Bath*

Purchased by Silver City Airways on 10/12/55

Leased to Air Kruise on 21/12/55

Returned to Silver City Airways on 01/10/57

Transferred to British United Air Ferries Ltd on 01/01/63

Withdrawn from use at Southend in
December 1964 and broken up in
November 1965

G-AHJJ – c/n 12742
Leased by Silver City Airways from The Bristol
Aeroplane Co. Ltd in December 1949
Returned in 1950

G-AHJP – c/n 12748
Purchased by Silver City Airways from
Compagnie Air Transport on 28/03/51 as
F-BENH
Sold to Air Outre-Mer, France, on 28/11/53

G-AICS – c/n 12762
Purchased by Silver City Airways from
British European Airways on 30/06/52
Leased to Manx Airlines Ltd until October
1957
Crashed and written-off at Winter Hill near
Bolton on 27/02/58

G-AICT – c/n 12763
Leased by Silver City Airways from The
Bristol Aeroplane Co. Ltd in April 1949
Returned in 1950

BRISTOL 170 FREIGHTER MK 32
G-AMWA – c/n 13073   *City of London*
Leased by Silver City Airways from The
Bristol Aeroplane Co. Ltd on 31/03/53
Purchased by Silver City Airways on 19/05/54
Transferred to Britavia on 03/04/62 and
leased back to Silver City Airways
Transferred to British United Air Ferries Ltd
on 01/01/63
Crashed and written-off at Guernsey on
24/09/63

G-AMWB – c/n 13127   *City of Salisbury*
Leased by Silver City Airways from
The Bristol Aeroplane Co.Ltd on
02/04/53
Purchased by Silver City Airways on
09/04/56
Transferred to Britavia on 03/04/62 and
leased back to Silver City Airways

Transferred to British United Air Ferries Ltd
on 01/01/63
Transferred to British Air Ferries Ltd on
01/10/67
Withdrawn from use at Lydd in March 1968
and broken up in April 1968

G-AMWC – c/n 13128   *City of Durham*
Leased by Silver City Airways from The
Bristol Aeroplane Co. Ltd on 09/05/53
Purchased by Silver City Airways on
30/08/57
Transferred to Britavia on 03/04/62 and
leased back to Silver City Airways
Transferred to British United Air Ferries Ltd
on 01/01/63
Withdrawn from use at Lydd in December
1964 and broken up in April 1967

**G-AMWD – c/n 13131   *City of Leicester/
City of Hereford***
Leased by Silver City Airways from
The Bristol Aeroplane Co. Ltd on
29/05/53
Purchased by Silver City Airways on
30/08/57
Leased to Compagnie Air Transport on
26/04/61 as F-BKBD

G-AMWE – c/n 13132   *City of York*
Leased by Silver City Airways from The Bristol
Aeroplane Co. Ltd on 11/06/53
Purchased by Silver City Airways on 30/08/57
Transferred to British United Air Ferries Ltd
on 01/01/63
Withdrawn from use at Lydd in December
1965 and broken up in April 1967

**G-AMWF – c/n 13133   *City of
Edinburgh/City of Coventry***
Leased by Silver City Airways from The
Bristol Aeroplane Co. Ltd on 23/06/53
Purchased by Silver City Airways on
30/08/57
Transferred to British United Air Ferries Ltd
on 01/01/63
Transferred to British Air Ferries Ltd on
01/10/67

Withdrawn from use at Lydd in November 1967 and broken up in March 1968

G-ANWG – c/n 1321   *City of Winchester*
Purchased by Silver City Airways on 23/06/54
Sold to Compagnie Air Transport in May 1961 as F-BKBG

G-ANWH – c/n 13212
Purchased by Silver City Airways on 06/07/54
Leased to Compagnie Air Transport in December 1962 as F-BLHH

G-ANWI – c/n 13213   *City of Glasgow*
Purchased by Silver City Airways on 23/07/54
Leased to Compagnie Air Transport in June 1961 as F-BKBI

G-ANWJ – c/n 13254   *City of Bristol*
Leased by Silver City Airways from The Bristol Aeroplane Co. Ltd on 01/06/56
Purchased by Silver City Airways on 28/09/56
Transferred to British United Air Ferries Ltd on 01/01/63
Transferred to British Air Ferries Ltd on 01/10/67
Withdrawn from use at Lydd in March 1968 and broken up in July 1970

G-ANWK – c/n 13259   *Fourteenth of July – Le Quatorze Juillet/City of Leicester*
Leased by Silver City Airways from The Bristol Aeroplane Co. Ltd on 19/06/56
Purchased by Silver City Airways on 05/07/56
Transferred to British United Air Ferries Ltd on 01/01/63
Transferred to British Air Ferries Ltd on 01/10/67
Withdrawn from use at Lydd in October 1969 and broken up in August 1970

G-ANWL – c/n 13260   *City of Worcester*
Purchased by Silver City Airways on 06/07/56
Crashed in Guernsey on 01/11/61

G-ANWM – c/n 13261   *City of Aberdeen*
Leased by Silver City Airways from The Bristol Aeroplane Co. Ltd on 19/07/56
Purchased by Silver City Airways on 30/04/57
Transferred to British United Air Ferries Ltd on 01/01/63
Transferred to British Air Ferries Ltd on 01/10/67
Leased to Compagnie Air Transport on 24/01/68 as F-BPIM
Returned on 26/11/69
Withdrawn from use and broken up at Lydd in October 1970

G-ANWN – c/n 13262   *City of Hull*
Leased by Silver City Airways from The Bristol Aeroplane Co. Ltd on 26/07/56
Purchased by Silver City Airways on 30/04/57
Transferred to British United Air Ferries Ltd on 01/01/63
Transferred to British Air Ferries Ltd on 01/10/67
Leased to Compagnie Air Transport on 04/03/68 as F-BPIN

DE HAVILLAND DH86 EXPRESS
G-ACZP – c/n 2321
Purchased by Lancashire Aircraft Corporation Ltd on 20/04/51
Transferred to Silver City Airways on 28/10/57
Sold to V.H. Bellamy (for Hampshire Aeroplane Club) on 21/02/58

DE HAVILLAND DH89A DRAGON RAPIDE
G-AKOE – c/n 6601
Purchased by Lancashire Aircraft Corporation Ltd on 26/05/49
Transferred to Silver City Airways 28/10/57
Sold to Hants & Sussex Aviation on 16/10/58

DE HAVILLAND DH90 DRAGONFLY
G-AEWZ – c/n 7555
Purchased by Silver City Airways on 19/07/50
Sold to V.H. Bellamy on 26/05/60

DE HAVILLAND DH104 DOVE 1

G-AIWF – c/n 04023
Purchased by British Aviation Services on
20/11/46
Transferred to Silver City Airways on
21/01/48
Sold to Commercial Air Services, South
Africa on 17/11/51

G-AKJP – c/n 04064
Purchased by Silver City Airways on
04/12/48
Sold to Iraq Petroleum Transport Co. Ltd on
17/01/51

G-AOYC – c/n 04065
Purchased by Silver City Airways on
25/02/59
Transferred to Morton Air Services Ltd on
01/04/64

DE HAVILLAND DH104 DOVE 2

G-AKJG – c/n 04071
Purchased by Silver City Airways in October
1947
Operated under private contract for Mrs V
Courtauld
Sold to Southern Rhodesia on 10/03/51

G-ANGE – c/n 04167
Leased by Silver City Airways in 1954 for
operations in Libya
Sold on 01/06/55

DE HAVILLAND DH114 HERON 1B

G-AOZM – c/n 14002 *City of Bradford*
Purchased by Silver City Airways on
10/04/57
Operated by Manx Airlines Ltd
Sold to Aircraft Leasing Co. Ltd on
11/12/59

G-AOZN – c/n 14005 *City of Belfast*
Purchased by Silver City Airways on
12/02/57
Operated by Manx Airlines Ltd
Sold to Aircraft Leasing Co. Ltd on
16/11/59

DOUGLAS DC-2-115B

ZS-DFX – c/n 1332
Leased by Silver City Airways (Libya) Ltd
during 1957

DOUGLAS C-47 DAKOTA

EI-ACG – c/n 4579
Leased by Silver City Airways from Aer
Lingus on 07/04/59
Returned on 28/10/60

EI-ACI – c/n 9036
Leased by Silver City Airways from Aer
Lingus on 11/03/59
Returned on 03/11/60

G-AKNB – c/n 9043 *City of Bradford*
Purchased by Silver City Airways on
11/12/59
Transferred to British United Airways Ltd
on 23/01/62

DOUGLAS C-47A DAKOTA

EI-ACK – c/n 19503
Leased by Silver City Airways from Aer
Lingus on 11/03/59
Returned on 09/02/60

EI-ACT – c/n 12471
Leased by Silver City Airways from Aer
Lingus on 12/03/59
Returned on 27/10/60

G-AIRG – c/n 25288
Purchased by British Aviation Services on
24/09/46
Transferred to Silver City Airways on
25/11/46
Sold to Burma Corporation on 30/03/48

G-AIRH – c/n 12445
Purchased by Britavia on 24/09/46
Transferred to Silver City Airways on
19/10/46
Transferred to British Aviation Services
(Air Charter and Exploration) in October
1948
Sold to Africair Ltd on 23/07/49

G-AIWC – c/n 13474 — *City of Tripoli/ City of Lincoln*

Purchased by Silver City Airways on 03/04/58 (named *City of Tripoli*)
Leased to Libyan Oil Co. Ltd on 30/10/59
Returned to Silver City Airways (named *City of Lincoln*)
Sold to Sabena on 14/02/62

G-AJAU – c/n 12433

Purchased by Silver City Airways on 18/11/46
Sold to Malayan Airways on 28/10/47

G-AJAV – c/n 12386 — *City of Hollywood*

Purchased by Silver City Airways on 09/01/47
Sold to General Electric Corporation, USA on 06/09/50

G-AJZD – c/n 12333

Purchased by British Aviation Services on 18/06/47
Transferred to Silver City Airways on 18/02/48
Sold to British Nederland Air Service on 22/03/48

G-AKII – c/n 12299

Leased by Silver City Airways from Cyprus Airways Ltd in February 1958
Returned in August 1958

G-ALFO – c/n 20401

Registered to Silver City Airways (Australia) Pty Ltd on 28/02/47 as VH–BHC
Transferred to the Zinc Corporation Ltd on 30/12/48 as G-ALFO
Sold to Standard Industries Corporation, USA on 22/12/50

G-ALPN – c/n 12158 — *City of Belfast*

Purchased by Silver City Airways on 17/11/59
Transferred to British United Airways Ltd on 23/01/62

G-ANLF – c/n 11979 — *City of Cambridge*

Purchased by Air Kruise on 20/04/55
Transferred to Silver City Airways on 28/10/57
Sold to Sabena on 01/09/61

DOUGLAS C-47B DAKOTA

G-AGND – c/n 26725

Leased by Silver City Airways from Cyprus Airways Ltd in February 1958
Returned in August 1958

G-AMJU – c/n 25925 — *City of Leeds*

Purchased by Silver City Airways on 04/03/58
Transferred to British United Airways Ltd on 23/01/62

G-AMPZ – c/n 32872 — *City of Dublin*

Purchased by British United Airways Ltd on 01/06/60
Transferred to Silver City Airways in March 1962
Transferred to British United Airways (Channel Islands) Ltd on 01/11/62

G-AMRA – c/n 26735

Leased by Silver City Airways from Starways Ltd in August 1959

G-AMVC – c/n 33390

Leased by Silver City Airways from BKS Air Transport Ltd on 14/04/1958
Returned on 17/09/58

G-AMWV – c/n 25600 — *City of Lancaster*

Purchased by Lancashire Aircraft Corporation Ltd in December 1952
Transferred to Silver City Airways on 28/10/57
Transferred to British United Airways Ltd on 23/01/62

G-AMYV – c/n 32943 — *City of Oxford*

Purchased by Silver City Airways on 01/04/53
Transferred to Silver City Airways (Libya) Ltd for remainder of 1953
Transferred to Air Kruise on 30/01/56

Transferred to Silver City Airways on
28/10/57
Transferred to British United Airways
(Channel Islands) Ltd on 01/11/62

G-AMYX – c/n 33042   *City of Rochester*

Purchased by Silver City Airways on
01/04/53
Transferred to Air Kruise on 30/01/56
Returned on 28/10/57
Transferred to British United Airways Ltd
23/01/62

G-AMZB – c/n 26980   *City of Guildford*

Purchased by Manx Airlines Ltd on
26/03/53
Transferred to Air Kruise on 06/11/56
Transferred to Silver City Airways on
28/10/57
Transferred to British United Airways Ltd
on 23/01/62

G-ANAE – c/n 26101   *City of Newcastle*

Purchased by Lancashire Aircraft
Corporation Ltd on 15/06/53
Transferred to Silver City Airways on
28/10/57
Transferred to British United Airways Ltd
on 23/01/62

DOUGLAS C-53D DAKOTA

G-AOBN – c/n 11711   *City of Canterbury*

Purchased by Air Kruise on 20/04/55
Transferred to Silver City Airways on
28/10/57
Transferred to British United Airways
(Channel Islands) Ltd on 01/11/62

DOUGLAS C-54B SKYMASTER

G-ALEP – c/n 18327

Leased by Silver City Airways from Mining
and Exploration Air Services Ltd on
21/01/49
Returned in April 1951

HANDLEY PAGE HP81 HERMES 4

G-ALDG – c/n HP81/8   *City of Chester*

Leased by Silver City Airways from CL Air
Surveys Ltd on 11/08/59
Returned on 16/10/59
Purchased by Silver City Airways from
Falcon Airways Ltd on 29/10/59
Withdrawn from use in October 1962

*(Fuselage used by British United Airways Ltd
for cabin crew training at Gatwick and now
preserved at Imperial War Museum, Duxford)*

G-ALDI – c/n HP81/10   *City of Coventry*

Purchased by Britavia on 19/06/54
Transferred to Silver City Airways in
September 1959
Withdrawn from use in October 1962 and
broken up at Stansted

G-ALDM – c/n HP81/14

Leased by Britavia from Air Safaris Ltd in
November 1956
Transferred to Silver City Airways on
15/06/59
Returned to Air Safaris Ltd on 13/10/59

G-ALDP – c/n HP81/17   *City of Truro*

Purchased by Britavia on 28/06/54
Transferred to Silver City Airways on
15/06/59
Withdrawn from use in October 1962 and
broken up at Stansted

G-ALDU – c/n HP81/21   *City of Gloucester*

Purchased by Britavia on 27/05/54
Leased to Kuwait Airways on 20/05/56
Returned on 07/12/56
Transferred to Silver City Airways in July
1959
Withdrawn from use in October 1962 and
broken up at Stansted

G-ALDX – c/n HP81/24

Purchased by Britavia on 31/05/54
Leased to Kuwait Airways on 29/05/56
Returned on 20/12/56

Transferred to Silver City Airways in August 1959

Withdrawn from use in November 1959 and broken up at Blackbushe

HUREL-DUBOIS HD34
F-BICU – c/n 07

Leased by Silver City Airways during 1959

LOCKHEED L-12A ELECTRA JUNIOR
G-AGWN – c/n 1275

Purchased by the Zinc Corporation Ltd on 12/06/50

Transferred to Silver City Airways (Australia) Pty Ltd 31/10/52

Sold in October 1957

LOCKHEED L-18H LODESTAR
G-AJAW – c/n 1954

Registered by British Aviation Services on 18/01/47

Transferred to Silver City Airways on 20/01/48

Sold to Sweden on 29/08/51

PERCIVAL P34 PROCTOR 3
G-ALFB – c/n H540

Purchased by Silver City Airways on 24/04/49

Sold to Algeria on 16/06/51

VICKERS 708 VISCOUNT
G-ARBY – c/n 010

Leased by Silver City Airways from Maitland Drewery Aviation Ltd in December 1961

Transferred to British United Airways Ltd in January 1962

G-ARER – c/n 012

Leased by Silver City Airways from Maitland Drewery Aviation Ltd in December 1961

Transferred to British United Airways Ltd in January 1962

G-ARGR – c/n 014

Leased by Silver City Airways from

Maitland Drewery Aviation Ltd in December 1961

Transferred to British United Airways Ltd in January 1962

WESTLAND-SIKORSKY S51 DRAGONFLY
G-ANLV – c/n WA/H/132

Leased by Silver City Airways during August 1954

APPENDIX 4

FLEET LIST – SOCIÉTÉ COMMERCIALE AÉRIENNE DU LITTORAL (SCAL) AND COMPAGNIE AIR TRANSPORT

BRISTOL 170 FREIGHTER MK I
F-BCJN – c/n 12788
Purchased by SCAL in July 1947
Crashed off Cartagena, Spain, on 16/10/47

BRISTOL 170 FREIGHTER MK 21
F-BECT – c/n 12798
Purchased by Compagnie Air Transport on 10/12/48
Sold to Silver City Airways on 01/04/52 as G-AIMH

F-BENC – c/n 12774
Purchased by Compagnie Air Transport on 26/08/48
Sold to Air Vietnam in January 1952

F-BEND – c/n 12773
Purchased by Compagnie Air Transport on 20/05/48
Sold to Silver City Airways in October 1951 as G-AIFM

F-BENF – c/n 12738
Purchased by Compagnie Air Transport on 01/04/48
Crashed near Tanezrouft, Algeria, on 28/07/50

F-BHVB – c/n 12731
Purchased by Compagnie Air Transport from Silver City Airways on 06/02/57 as G-AGVB
Crashed and written-off at Le Touquet on 04/11/58

BRISTOL 170 FREIGHTER MK 21E
F-BCJM – c/n 12787
Purchased by SCAL on 26/07/47
Sold to Shackleton Aviation Ltd in May 1957

F-BENG – c/n 12812
Purchased by Compagnie Air Transport on 18/03/48
Crashed and written-off at Los Barrios, Spain, on 11/04/48

F-BENH – c/n 12748
Purchased by Compagnie Air Transport on 27/05/48
Sold to Silver City Airways on 28/03/51 as G-AHJP

BRISTOL 170 FREIGHTER MK 31
F-BFUO – c/n 13076
Purchased by SCAL from Aer Lingus in October 1956
Leased to Air Fret
Sold to Aer Turas on 21/11/66

BRISTOL 170 FREIGHTER MK 32

F-BKBD – c/n 13131

Leased by Compagnie Air Transport from
Silver City Airways on 26/04/61

Returned to British United Air Ferries Ltd
on 07/01/63 as G-AMWD

Withdrawn from use at Lydd in December
1965 and broken up at Southend in April
1967

F-BKBG – c/n 13211   *Quatorze Juillet*

Purchased by Compagnie Air Transport
from Silver City Airways in May 1961 as
G-ANWG

Withdrawn from use at Lydd in November
1967 and broken up in March 1968

F-BKBI – c/n 13213   *Onze Novembre*

Leased by Compagnie Air Transport from
Silver City Airways in June 1961 as
G-ANWI

Withdrawn from use at Lydd in January
1968 and broken up in April 1968

F-BLHH – c/n 13212   *Dix-Huit Juin*

Leased by Compagnie Air Transport from
Silver City Airways in December 1962 as
G-ANWH

Damaged beyond repair and written-off at
Le Touquet on 11/09/69

F-BPIM – c/n 13262

Leased to Compagnie Air Transport from
British Air Ferries Ltd 24/01/68 as
G-ANWM

Returned on 26/11/69

F-BPIN – c/n 13263

Leased to Compagnie Air Transport from
British Air Ferries Ltd 04/03/68 as
G-ANWN

Withdrawn from use at Lydd in April 1969
and broken up in August 1970

APPENDIX 5

COMPANY LINEAGE

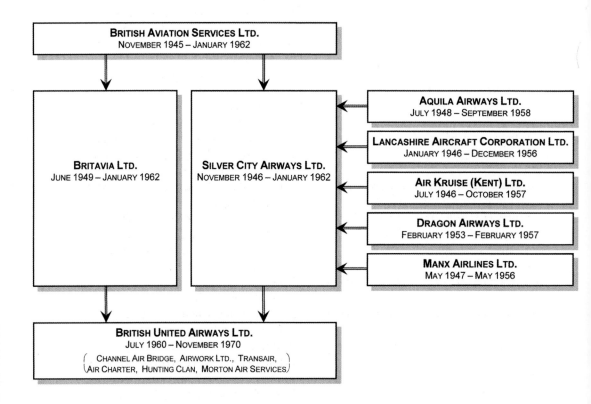

INDEX